Wire Java:
....
Your Hot Workbook Guide
To Selling Your Jewelry!

Wire Java:
Your Hot Workbook Guide To Selling Your Jewelry!

by Mitzi McCartha

Wire Java: Your Hot Workbook Guide To Selling Your Jewelry!

P.O. Box 150522
Ogden, UT 84415

©2010 Wire-Sculpture.com
First Printing July 2010

All rights reserved. No part of this book may be reproduced or transmitted in any form or by any means, electronic, mechanical, photocopying, recording, or otherwise, without witten permission of the publisher.

For information on obtaining permission for reprints and excerpts, contact customerservice@wire-sculpture.com.

Printed in the USA
Cover design and layout by Chris Compton (wire-sculpture.com)
Edited by Dale 'Cougar' Armstrong and Rose Marion
Cover photography by Al Alvaro

This book is dedicated to the memory of my father, Ralph DeHowitt, who was always a fan of the entrepreneur. His firm belief in being your own boss has been the catalyst for what I am today. Thanks, Dad, you gave the best advice ever!

Acknowledgements

I would like to thank Dale Armstrong for suggesting that I create a special book that assists wire artists in selling their work. Her support in this endeavor will make the business life of the crafter much easier. I would also like to extend a special thank you to Alec Day and the great staff at Wire-Sculpture for their willingness to support customers in their business endeavors by offering this book for their use.

Table of Contents

Preface *1*

Chapter One *3*
Something's Brewing: Getting Started

Chapter Two *7*
Wake Up and Smell the Coffee! Some Things You Should Know

Chapter Three *33*
100% Fresh Brew: Taking the Plunge

Chapter Four *45*
Mellow, Mild, or Nutty? Creating Your Line

Chapter Five *49*
Getting Down to the Grind: Pricing, Somebody's Gotta Do It!

Chapter Six *57*
The Writing's On the Bag: Marketing Materials

Chapter Seven *67*
Java Jolt! Ideas on Where to Sell Your Jewelry

Chapter Eight *87*
Spilling the Beans: On Marketing Your Jewelry

Chapter Nine *105*
Espresso Kick: Principles and Elements of Design

Chapter Ten *111*
One for the Road! Conclusion

Appendix *114*
Wire Chart

Resources *116*

About the Author *118*

Preface

Having been involved in several businesses over the last fifteen years, I have found one attribute in common; one has to competitively price goods and services sold! Pricing seems to be one of the most difficult decisions business owners make. Due to market locations, products and services offered, competition, and customer demand, there becomes a list of variables to consider when pricing.

Some markets allow the use of proven formulas, while others rely on values obtained in their region for similar goods and services. The final decision ultimately comes down to determining the price you can receive from the sale of your product. When working with wire, for example, the other issue to consider is labor! Depending on pieces you craft and materials involved, the cost of goods can be lower at times, but the labor for an intricate piece can be quite intensive.

In this book I address this as well as other issues influencing price: 1) Where are you located? 2) Who are your competitors and what are they charging? 3) How strong is the demand for your type of item? The above points are just a few of the many questions to address as you set up your business to market and sell your jewelry. However, you will learn that pricing, though a big part of your business responsibility, is not the only activity in which you will engage. This book reviews multiple aspects of setting up your jewelry business, and the various forms at the end of each chapter will guide you through every step along the way. Even if you are considering other crafting activities, this book can help you apply the principles needed to assist in creating a profitable business. Reading this book will answer most of your questions and, hopefully, a few that you may have not considered. Ultimately your goal is to be pleasantly surprised by the profits you can potentially reap by offering your unique and wonderful products! With the help from this book, you will without a doubt be well on your way!

Chapter One
Something's Brewing: Getting Started

So, you want to start selling your jewelry! Perhaps you remember the "A-Ha" moment you had when you began to consider selling your work. You wore your pieces to work or church, got tons of compliments, and people exclaimed, "Oh, I want one! Can you make me one with a blue stone instead of a green one? Please add some dangle drops too. Oh, and can you add some curly-q's for fun?" After this continued over a period of months, the light bulb in your head came on, and you thought, "You know, I should start selling my designs. I think I could make some money at this…"

Does this scenario sound familiar? Perhaps your story goes a little differently, but you've ended up at the same fork in the road where you decide whether to continue your craft as a fun, light-hearted hobby, or take it to the next level—that of becoming an entrepreneur and designer.

Sounds exciting, doesn't it? But hold on a minute! If you are strongly leaning towards creating a business for yourself with your crafted jewelry as the product, there will be some preliminary business activities you must address, such as getting a business license and obtaining a sales and use tax number. As you progress in your set-up, you will find out that there's more you will need to do than just creating and designing jewelry. There are hosts of marketing and other production plans that you will have to consider. In the following chapters, I hope to address some of these procedures.

I can speak from personal experience. In the beginning, making jewelry as a hobby was not on my list of things to do.

The thoughts of delving into wire jewelry totally scared me to death and sent me running in the opposite direction! Creating a business with it was even farther from my mind. I actually stumbled on jewelry-crafting out of necessity, when I was trying to create a special bracelet for a project I had undertaken. I met a couple of people who could make jewelry and indicated that they could make me what I wanted. However, I never heard back from them. It suddenly dawned on me one day that I could most likely make my own bracelet! With enough perseverance, I finally accomplished my goal of finishing a bracelet that not only fit but also provided me with the design and functionality I needed. After that, I was hooked.

After experiencing the jewelry-crafting world as a hobby for over three years and selling my jewelry in some local boutiques, I finally opened my first retail bead shop in 2005. It wasn't until 2006 that I was introduced to wire. I had finally gotten up the courage to try it and was invited to take a class with Dale Armstrong, a renowned wire artist. After spending an intense weekend learning about the beginning wire basics, tools, and techniques, I came away with some splendid knowledge with which to create my own designs. I was then able to make some unique pieces that I sold in my shop. I found that beads and stones are great accents for wire pieces, and that I was able to set myself apart from other crafters who sold their jewelry. Working in wire allows one to enter a special world that lends itself well to unique creativity that is not readily found in more traditional, basic jewelry-crafting. Now that I own a shop, I don't have the time to make and sell my pieces as much anymore, but I love the world of hand-crafted jewelry—especially wire! It's also rewarding for me as I see customers grow and develop their talents.

Not everyone will end up owning their own retail shop, which is another whole ballgame, but you may decide to take your jewelry crafting hobby up a notch. Many of the suggestions I reference in this book have not only come from my own experience, but from others to whom I have spoken during my tenure in the jewelry world. Just sharing some of these marketing ideas without some brief discussion on business basics won't help you fully; it will be necessary to review some of these issues so you can at least be aware of them. I have also created this book to be a beginning workbook where you can list your ideas, note contacts, marketing outlets, and other information you wish to record. There are worksheets at the end of each chapter, and you can use them as beginning templates. A Resources listing is noted at the end of the book.

The Coffee's Percolating!

Do you think you're ready to make a business of selling your jewelry? Ask yourself the following questions:

1. Am I getting compliments on jewelry I created?
2. Are people asking me to make something similar for them?
3. Do I enjoy making pieces for other people?
4. Do I like the thrill and challenge of designing for others?
5. Do I even have the time to do more crafting if there is a demand?
6. Do I like the idea of running the ins and outs of a business, and doing all the tasks required, knowing that actual jewelry production may be the last part of the equation?
7. Will I have the desire and ability to market my jewelry?
8. Am I a "people-person?"

If you answered "Yes" to any of these questions, then you may be well on your way to creating a fun and rewarding business for yourself. If you answered "No" to any of these, what the heck! Read this book anyway, as it may reduce some of your anxiety or fears about plunging into the world of small business. The materials in this book will help you in the future if you change your mind, or if you would like to pursue your jewelry craft just to support your hobby. If anything, you will want to take a hard look at what you really want to achieve in regard to your craft. I have a customer who blatantly told me that she prefers to make jewelry for herself and is simply not ready to face the challenge of designing for others, though they beg her to. I have other customers who merely wish to sell their pieces to co-workers, friends, and family, making just enough to support their hobby. That's ok, too. For those of you who want to make a full-time career out of selling your wire jewelry and pursue this decision on a deeper level, you will have some fun yet challenging tasks ahead of you. You will have an opportunity to be creative not only with your jewelry designs, but also in other areas as well.

Changing a hobby into a business means that you have decided that you also enjoy being a business person and an entrepreneur. I've been in business activities since 1996, which include antiques and gift dealer, seller on eBay, and wedding video producer. With all of these ventures, I had to be involved with business activities such as marketing, bookkeeping, and production, as well as dealing with the products or service I was actually selling. Be honest with yourself and most important of all: don't burn yourself out on an activity that you enjoy because you did something you were not ready for at a moment in time. In the meantime, arm yourself with some knowledge that will help make your life easier and more rewarding. So sit back, grab a cup of your favorite java blend and read on!

Chapter Two
Wake Up and Smell the Coffee! Some Things You Should Know

Ok, so you must have decided that you want to know more about starting your own jewelry business, or else you wouldn't be reading this book, would you? Making a decision to actually pursue a dream or any idea you have is always a little scary at first. Obviously you are asking yourself, "Do I have the skill to do this?" or "Will there be others out there who like what I do?" or "Will I have time to do this?" But have you considered other questions such as: How will I market my product?" "How will I fill and track orders?" "What will I do if I become ill and can't meet a deadline?" or "What if I get so many requests I can't fill them all?" Of course there are the legal steps you must take, such as getting a business license and a Sales and Use Tax Number (so you can buy wholesale and not pay sales tax). If the questions above seem a little overwhelming, then you are experiencing the first twinge of reality: changing a hobby into an actual business.

There is a big difference between the two, if you haven't started to figure that out already! A hobby is something light-hearted and fun—something you can do when you feel like it. Making a living really is not an issue at this point. A business is not a hobby anymore, though it can still be lots of fun. However, you pursue it to also make a profit. It will actually place several responsibilities on you if you want to be successful. If you have a "go get 'em" attitude, or you enjoy a challenge and don't mind hard work, then you will be on the right track toward a fun and rewarding business for yourself. I have listed some top issues I believe need to be considered when changing a hobby into a business.

1. Time

In our world today, there are so many things that compete for this commodity. Sometimes "Time" is all you have, and sometimes there just doesn't seem to be enough of it. But there is one thing for sure. You will need time for your business. A friend's husband once said to me that having a successful business is "90% perspiration and 10% inspiration." Now, that may sound strange to you if you thought that having a jewelry business would let you play in beads and findings all day and that all you would do is design and just have a ball! Honestly, I agree that there is truly more background work into the planning, marketing, and maintaining of the business than there is of actual design work.

For example, in my business, customers have this notion that all I do is sit around and make jewelry all day long. Nothing could be farther from the truth! I'm busy assisting customers, ordering and displaying more merchandise, creating a newsletter, or updating a website. Little time is spent on making jewelry for me, though I can sometimes make a little to sell. So, what does this mean for you? Discipline! You must have discipline and excellent organizational skills to help you out. No watching television in the evenings after getting home from work. You may be spending a nice sunny weekend creating a catalog, filling orders, coming up with new designs, working a show or creating brochures, just to name a few of the many activities in which you will be engaged. What will you do when there is a choice to be made between filling an order that has to go out immediately and attending a family event for the evening? You will need to take a look at your emotional scales and see which weighs in as more important, watching your favorite TV shows, doing family activities, or becoming your own boss.

These questions are only meant to make you think, not make an on-the-spot value judgment. It all goes back to the question of, "Will you have the time to maintain and develop your business?" It will take some sacrificing to make this business work, and you will need to involve your family in helping you make proper arrangements for time to work your business and time to devote to other areas of your life. Do plan time for rest and relaxation, or you will burn yourself out quickly. Getting your family's support and buy-in is imperative, or you may be doomed from the beginning. So don't start off on the wrong track only to suddenly realize that you don't have the time, energy, or support to do all that needs to be done to make your business a successful one.

2. Finding Your Niche

You'll hear everyone saying that you need a niche. This isn't hearsay, it's the truth! Finding a unique and niche market is important if you want to stand out. Let's admit it, jewelry is everywhere, and many are doing it these days. Is there an area you can tap into that will fulfill your creative wishes and still create a product that can be enjoyed by many? There are several areas to consider that you may not have thought about. In Chapter 7, some of these ideas will be presented in more detail. Perhaps you already have an idea of what you would like to do, and that's great! You've answered one of the biggest questions already. The goal you want to achieve is to set yourself apart from others and do something different from everyone else. So get creative and look at all your possible options. Are you currently involved in some type of hobby or organization where you could create jewelry reflecting a mascot, image, or theme? If not, start thinking about areas of personal interest, or get some input from friends, family, and acquaintances. I find that most people are always ready to have their ideas heard! You may want to pay attention to what they suggest because they may hit on a neat idea that puts money in your pocket and becomes a source of revenue for you.

My first arena for jewelry making was bridal. Because I had previously been involved in producing wedding videos, bridal was the most familiar to me. My husband and a good friend, who owned a bridal store at the time, encouraged me to create a bridal line. The nice part about this niche is that it allowed many options within it, focusing not only on just the bride, but creating for bridesmaids, flower girls, and mother of the bride. The best thing you can do is find an avenue that will provide you enjoyment, while creating meaningful pieces to the prospective buyers. In this situation, everyone wins!

3. Education

Knowledge is golden, and it can be a big key to success, from knowing which markets to go after, to learning who the right contacts are to get you into certain shops and shows to sell your jewelry. Educating yourself in your industry, networking, and learning new marketing techniques are vital to making your business viable and successful. Marketing is itself an art and an industry, and a little more information will be devoted to this subject in Chapter 8. Do spend some time in doing your homework, learning about the materials going into your product, learning where to sell in your community or surrounding areas, and learning how to network with other artisans or businesses. These all help get your name out to the public and your work into the appropriate shops and galleries. Get on the Internet and determine if there are any small business networks you can join in your area. These organizations may charge a membership fee, but the price may pay off in dividends regarding sales. An additional plus is that you have a peer group with whom you can share ideas, and they can be a great sounding board when you need it!

I have also spent time researching ways to build my business and have engaged in countless hours reading marketing and sales books. Likewise, I have taken the time to talk to other small business owners who could offer support and advice on promoting my business. These people are great referral sources and respected friends. They also are small business owners who understand the need to market and promote their products. We share common ground when it comes to creating ideas for better customer service or discovering which promotional activity yields the best results. You get therapeutic support and wonderful ideas from networking. Get out and "pound the pavement" and be aware of your environment, so you can have a burst of inspiration to create a promotional item for your current line! Study fashion magazines, clothing catalogs, and know what's in the department stores. All this takes time, and you have to decide if you want to put energy and effort into this. I personally find this area fascinating and rewarding and it will keep you on your toes if you are serious about promoting and building your business. Always be looking for the next idea for a new line when the old ones fade out. Keep educated and abreast of your industry.

4. Vendor Sources

Where to purchase materials is important for those trying to produce and sell their jewelry designs. With the Internet, local bead shows, and community bead shops readily available, you will find a plethora of great sources for creating your lines, as well as comfortable pricing that allows you to make a profit.

First of all, as a shop owner, I always advocate trying out your local bead shops. Why? Because you can touch and feel the merchandise before you buy, as well as match up the materials to the projects you are working on. Check for pricing. Some shops actually do have acceptable prices, and may provide some volume discount schedules. Best of all, you can take your goods home right away. The staff can also provide wonderful input and may be a resource for creating wonderful pieces. However, if you are reproducing a particular item over and over again, you may need to buy in bulk. You can ask a local bead shop owner if they can obtain the items you need and if they would be willing to help you get bulk quantities. You may be required to put a deposit down for the merchandise to ensure your purchase. After all, what you are looking for may not be their regular stock item, and they are considering your request a special order. If they are unable to do this, then you may have to use an Internet vendor from whom you can order in large quantities as many times as you need to.

There are some fabulous Internet sources for wire and related materials, and the sites are easy to navigate, the dimensions of stones and wire gauges are clear, and the myriad of offerings is staggering. Wire-Sculpture.com is one of my favorites for suggesting to customers. It is the premier site for obtaining materials related to wire and other jewelry crafting needs. The selection is broad, pictures and descriptions are clear, and the customer service is beyond reproach. You can also get tutorials and other crafting guides to help you along with your creativity. Once you find an Internet vendor such as this, you will find them an invaluable resource.

Another source for materials is the local bead shows. If you search the Internet, you can learn which ones come to your area. You can also stop by your local bead shop and they can most likely tell you when the shows occur. Shows come only a few times a year and can be a valuable source for materials; however, you still may be stuck with the indecision of just how much to buy. Another problem you may face is that you will not be able to go back and buy the same item again when you need it. The vendors may not be able to provide much insight into jewelry creations, but hey, "parts is parts" and you're sure to find a lot of them during a show!

Ok, now it's time for my soapbox speech regarding vendors and your new position as the designer. First of all, you will definitely need a Sales and Use Tax Certification. This certificate containing your number is the starting point in establishing you as a business, and it allows you to purchase materials tax-free. Keep several copies of your certificate on hand, because shows and vendors are now being required to have a copy of these certificates of resale for their files. Some shows will not even let you in unless you have this. Having this number suddenly makes you feel important, doesn't it? You're a business now, and so you're off to find some great things to include in your product line that you've spent so much time in creating. It's okay to politely ask the vendors if they have any special pricing for those with tax numbers. Usually they are only too happy to share their pricing structure with you. As a business they are hoping to have you as a customer for a long time. But look out—here's when the "moment of truth" occurs. The vendor sets terms that do not immediately set well with your pocket book. What's a designer to do? First of all do not, under any circumstance, argue with vendors by stating that you are a small company and cannot follow their terms. Numerous times I have heard vendors complain about dealing with designers. They are weary of designers claiming to be a business, wanting wholesale pricing, but only buying one or two items. If you are going to be a business, then you need to act like one! Either play by their rules or don't play. There, I've said it! Now I'll get off my soapbox and give you a couple of ways to deal with the "untimely" news!

You can look at the situation like this: You see a vendor's sign indicating you will receive fifty percent off five hundred dollars of selected merchandise. You make your selection, and guess what? You actually pay two hundred fifty dollars. Not bad when you hear it that way—you actually got your merchandise much cheaper. If, however, you still cannot pay the price even with the discount, smile nicely, nod your head, and say, "Okay, thank you very much" or "Thank you, I'll keep that in mind," and slowly walk away. Please remember that it takes time to build relationships with vendors to such a level that they begin to make concessions for you or give you special little deals. One of my guest teachers is a national designer who works in wire. She said it took her eight years to finally reach a point with her wire vendor before they would let her have any amount of wire for the maximum price break. The relationship also works the other way. This means you will need to find vendors who not only carry the items you need but who are also willing to work with you and your needs. This can be anything from payment methods and schedules to assisting you in selecting merchandise. For example, we have vendors we can merely call by phone and ask them to send us merchandise based on our price range, color, and category type. They are only too happy to assist, and their products usually sell well as they know what sells best to the public. You have to earn vendors' trust and respect for you as a business. This is not as hard to do as it is timely; it pays off in the end when you will be greatly rewarded by a pleasant and successful relationship.

On a final note, regarding bead shows, many of you have heard about the show held in Tucson every winter. You will hear everyone telling you that this is the show you need to attend, as there are actually multiple shows being held throughout the city. Vendors come from all over to sell their goods and, yes, you can get some good deals. However, consider the expense incurred with travel, food, and lodging (which can be very expensive when the show is on). Unless you either live near the area or have thousands of dollars to spend, your good deals will be voided out by expenses that you have to recoup if you want to make a profit. That's why I suggest shows that are closer, "in your own back yard." You can still find some good vendors that will sell to you at affordable pricing so you can make some money. This is just my two cents worth, and you have to make the decision on what you can afford.

5. Production

Now it's time for the other "10%" of the business I mentioned earlier—the design and production of the goods. That's not to say you won't spend any time on actually putting your products together or coming up with some new designs. After all, you must have something to sell! Labor is an area that can break your bank if you don't put some planning and thought into how much time it will take you to produce each piece. When it comes to wire work, this can be a tricky area. Certain pieces can be very intricate and so labor-intensive that it simply may not be very profitable to make them so much. Other styles you create can be less intricate, and the more you make the pieces, the faster you create them. You can then make a profit more easily. Based on your niche, income of your potential clientele, and demand for the jewelry you create, you will have to determine if you want more specialized pieces, but fewer of them, or if you want to appeal to a broader moderate-income market and produce larger quantities of simply-constructed pieces. There is no "right way," and more is not always better; the goal here is to make you aware. Again, some items are just not feasible to make because the labor is too intense. You could have difficulty in getting your market value for the piece.

What do you do if you suddenly have orders coming at you from all directions? This can be overwhelming and scary. After all it's only you doing this—you're a one person show. First, be wary of setting unrealistic deadlines. This can make both parties feel bad. The buyer then doesn't trust you to get the merchandise to them in a timely manner. You are then left feeling inadequate, which can dent your self-confidence. Talk with your buyers and determine deadlines on the front end. It will spare you heartache in the end. Are you taking on too many avenues? Don't spread yourself thin. It's better to narrow your market and do it well instead of putting yourself in the position of operation overload. Don't be afraid to say no to certain projects, and do give realistic time-frames to prospective buyers up front.

While certain jewelry-crafting mediums lend themselves to having "hired help," wire artistry is mostly out of that picture. Apart from simple wire loops or wrapped coils, it is strongly recommended you refrain from trying to teach someone wire artistry techniques just to speed up the process. These techniques should be taught by an experienced wire artist who teaches professionally, and should not be attempted by you, the designer. There is so much more that goes into a project constructed of wire, than simply placing beads on a wire and crimping the ends after adding a clasp, for example. Perfecting wire techniques takes time, practice, and dedication to the craft. Also, when it comes to items constructed of wire, your customers want and expect these pieces to be made by you personally, not some crew that works with you. Wire pieces tend to command such a personal aspect from the artist—their time, technique, attention, creativity, and pride in what they do. If working in wire is your medium of choice, you may have a policy that you do not engage in production work (i.e. making 40 or 50 pieces of something!).

What happens if you suddenly become ill and can't make it to the craft show you've been planning to attend? This is the time to see if some nice friends of yours are willing to pitch in and help. You may find that they are only too eager to help, and the thoughts of participating in a show will be an exciting venture for them. If they are working a show, you will need to contact the appropriate coordinators to see about getting approval for your assistants to be there in your place. This should not pose a problem; the coordinators just need to be aware. If you are just trying to fill an order for a buyer, contact them immediately to discuss a revised deadline, or at least make them aware that someone will be dropping off the merchandise in your place. There is some training involved here, but that's part of being in business for yourself. Good help is hard to find, but when you do, it makes your life a whole lot easier.

Last, but not least, you will need to make items of nice quality. Remember, you are not a machine, and the jewelry you make is hand-crafted. Not every little twist or loop is going to be perfect; however, there is absolutely no excuse for greatly uneven loops, sloppy wire wraps, bindings, or sharp edges that could scratch and injure someone. A guest instructor shared with me that one of her students was so eager to try to sell her jewelry that she quickly made her pieces with little regard to her technique. She also tried to sell these pieces before she was technically skilled enough to create quality merchandise. As a result, one of her customers cut herself on a ring due to a wire sticking out! You want your products to be things of beauty and a joy to wear, not be a weapon against the wearer! Customers are savvy these days, and they pay more attention to detail than you think. If they are paying premium prices for their special pieces, they should at least receive something that's nicely finished. Do not get in a hurry and try to whip out items as fast as you can. The quality of the final product will show, and believe me, it won't be pretty; you'll have a hard sell on your hands. Sit down in your quiet work area, get into your "Zen" mode (I call it) and take your time. It's always been my experience that the more technically skilled you become, the more the appropriate speed comes. Don't force this.

There, enough said! Now go forth and create!

6. Marketing

Now here is an area that is a major stumbling block for most people, even for those who make this art their everyday livelihood. Great marketing skills are not for the faint at heart, and it really means putting yourself out there to get accepted, or worst of all, rejected. But don't despair; you won't die of shame if you are told no. Actually, I've heard that the more nos you get, the closer you are to getting the yes you really want! I'll spend a little more time in the marketing arena in Chapter 8. However, you need to know that turning your craft into a business means that you will have to market your business. There is no exception to this. You will have to pound the pavement and seek out buyers. If you are shy, learning to market is a great way to overcome this problem. There are marketing books and seminars to teach you how to improve your skills as well as provide some advice on how to choose your markets and address the roadblocks to the decision makers. Join a local Toastmasters group if you would like to improve your speaking skills.

If you find you don't have enough time to market, you may actually consider a sales representative to help sell your jewelry. In Dallas and Atlanta, to name a couple of places, there are large showrooms housing a multitude of items for sale. These range from jewelry to furniture and accessories. You can check with showrooms, or the market place staff to determine if there are available representatives who may want to show your line to vendors. In my area, the Atlanta Market Place is the entity where I might start searching for a representative. The nice thing about using a sales representative is that they travel to different regions as well as participate in certain shows. This means they are out with the public and have a high likelihood of finding buyers for your jewelry. You will need to meet with them and discuss their experience level, their interest in representing another product line in addition to the ones they already have, and how payments will be made. Experienced representatives may also help provide some insight into how to offer a line. They also have several connections and avenues by which to present your products as they are always in the showrooms and on the road meeting with and seeking out new buyers. Perhaps they will find some buyers for you. Some avenues are harder to penetrate than others. High end galleries or specialty artisan shops are looking for certain items that are very unique in style as well as show off an impeccable level of quality and craftsmanship. You will have to determine if you have the skill set or the artistic flair to meet their needs. Many of them are always looking for new artisans and new items. This is where unique, signature twists and designs come in handy, and wire is a perfect medium to help set you apart from other artisans. Pieces rendered in wire tend to have a creativity that cannot be readily matched by other jewelry-crafting techniques. Overall it's not impossible to get your foot into a nice shop or gallery, but just be aware that this is a different level than selling items to your friends and office co-workers, who already know you and have a certain bond with you and may be more overall forgiving.

7. Presentation

When you do decide to participate in a show, you will need to spend some time and funds on displays, lighting, and other hardware to make your area a fun and comfortable place to shop. This can sometimes be an expensive venture, but if you shop wisely, you can still find some fixtures at affordable prices. Outlet and display stores can offer decorative accent pieces that fit your budget. Why is presentation and display so important? Sometimes the packaging or set-up makes the item even more attractive to buy. Have you ever been inside a really neat boutique or gorgeous gift shop? Pay attention to the way the displays are positioned and what they hold. Think about how the atmosphere makes you feel; the "eye candy" you see sends a subliminal message that screams, "Buy me!" Pretty mirrors or statues make great earring, necklace, and bracelet holders. I once saw a vendor at a craft show who placed her jewelry on silver trays filled with rice and coffee beans. That was such a novel idea, not to mention the great aroma from the coffee beans! You can turn plastic bowls into risers when a nice cloth is placed over them. In creating attractive displays, you are also engaged in a form of marketing your wares, and women (and even the men) love looking at pretty things.

Make sure all your pieces have prices on them and that they are displayed for viewing ease and access. Though there are some people that love rummaging through things, I find most people appreciate cutting to the chase and being able to handle and review merchandise in the easiest way possible. Bring extra lighting to show off your items. I find there are many of us who have an "ostrich" instinct. We immediately go to what's sparkly and eye-catching, and nothing helps jewelry sparkle like good lighting. Raise your tables higher if you need to. Leaning too much can cause back strain and fatigue your customer, and you don't want that. You want them to stay and shop a while! In my shop, most of my merchandise is out there so people can touch and feel the items. The lighting is also very bright, and the main reason why people love the shop is because everything is well displayed and well-lit, not to mention there is a wide variety of items from which to select. As a good friend once told me that people feel a sense of obligation to buy if they touch something long enough. If you are showing your pieces to a buyer in a gallery or boutique, consider investing in a nice jewelry roll, where you can show multiple pieces at once. This shows you are prepared, take pride in your work, and are a professional. If certain pieces are best shown off on a bust or other display, bring it along if it's feasible. When it comes to presentation, sometimes you're not selling the "steak" as much as you are the "sizzle!"

8. Delivery

Basically, this concept is a pretty simple one, but I am still amazed at how unreliable people are, even those who pay lip service to the idea that they want to sell products they have crafted. For example, I have had the experience of giving an order to an eager artist, only to never hear from them again! In other situations, the artist followed through with the first order, but oddly, they never tried to get another one. If you want your business to be successful, it is imperative that you follow through on filling your customer's request. Even if this means juggling household duties, you will have to take the time to live up to your promise, fill the order, and deliver the goods. (You did remember to get family support, didn't you?) There should be no major excuses not to get items to a buyer, unless it's illness, emergency, or other acts of God.

Now that you have decided that you are reliable and really want your business to prosper, you've made the items and filled the order. It's time then to get it to the right person. Timely delivery is essential in gaining your buyers' trust. They are counting on your getting them their merchandise, whether the order is for an individual, shop, or gallery. Their goal is to have unique and wonderful products in their shops, meaningful tokens for others to keep a very long time. Don't disappoint either buyer! If you want to leave a more lasting impression, you may want to consider how you package your pieces. Unfortunately, bags and tissues usually end up in the trash. What a waste. You didn't get these items free, and they are part of your overhead costs. Why not get more "bang for the buck," and find pretty printed bags or those with an unusual design. You can always attach a cute hand-made tag that can be easily removed. The owner can then use the bag to package a gift for someone else. Pretty organza bags or silk pouches are even nicer and can be a means of storing jewelry. Nice pouches and bags are also less likely to be thrown in the trash. If you have knotted a strand of pearls for an individual customer, you may consider placing the strand in a stylish presentation box. The recipient will remember this forever! Your delivery style and packaging can also be your signature. In my business, I have cute decorative cellophane bags, and I get comments on them every time. One of my friends laughingly tells customers, "This is our new bag of the month." The bag also serves as a reminder to the customer where they got their merchandise. You can get packaging materials rather inexpensively if you do some research. The more you buy in bulk, the better the rate you get. Give someone that extra touch by which to remember you.

9. Legal Issues

This is definitely not the fun part of running a business, but it's far less fun to have state and federal authorities after you, that's for sure! Please do not take anything I say in this section as legal advice because I am no tax accountant or an attorney. You will need one of these professionals assisting you with your taxes and giving you advice on what's appropriate not only at a federal level but also at your state level. If you do decide that you are ready to go into business, I would recommend first meeting with a tax advisor or other professional appropriately deemed to give correct information on what you will need in order to get started as a business. Make a list of questions so that you won't forget an item of importance. What I will share with you here briefly outlines the top three items of which you will need to be aware.

A. Business License

The first point of order is to get a Business License if you are selling merchandise. In my research there was the question of "Do I always need a business license for what I am doing?" Most every answer pointed to "Yes," with the exception of very few service-oriented arenas. Most states want you to be registered as a business with the intent of making a profit. That's what sets you apart from a hobby! You will have to pay taxes on your business. In Tennessee, where I have my shop, we do this once a year when we renew our business license. The form directs you on how to do this. Don't be overwhelmed, you won't be paying thousands or millions of dollars unless you are a huge business empire. It's great to think big, but be realistic for now. Your County Clerk may be the starting point in your state to apply for a business license. Many states have license, tax forms and other business information available online, so it may be as simple as getting on your computer. You may need a Business License to participate in certain craft or vendor shows or to sell your items to certain businesses.

    I had a customer who was asked to create an item addressing Breast Cancer Awareness for a company for which she worked. These items were to be given as gifts to the employees to show appreciation for all their hard work and dedication to the company. She came up with here design idea, purchased her materials, and started to work, only to be told in the middle of the process that the company was unable to purchase the items from her because she did not have a business license! It appeared that the company could only write their purchase off as doing business only if they made a purchase from another business! Talk about a big let-down. Luckily she found other customers who were only too happy to buy her nice products. Whew, saved by the bell! Many shops and galleries want to do business only from legitimate manufacturers and businesses owners, so get a license and be the real deal.

B. Personalty Tax

Here's a "secret" that appears to be a big one for many people in business – Personalty Tax. No, that's not "Personality": it is "Personalty." That's what they call this in my state. This tax is paid on the items it takes to run your business. Different types of businesses pay different types of taxes, and Personalty Tax is one you may be paying on yours. Once a year, you will have to list all the items you use to run your business: desk, tables, chairs, computer, and fixtures. I will not attempt to list everything that you will put on this form. Contact your assessor or tax payer's office, and they will be glad to give information concerning this tax, as well as how to fill out the forms. Don't think that just because you are home-based that you are exempt. When you apply for a license, this may clue the Assessor's Office to contact you. Don't panic, this is not difficult to address, and again, you won't be paying thousands of dollars unless you are a huge business. You aren't Tiffany's yet! Also a word of caution—do not let your tax advisor tell you to let this tax be "forced". If one is "forced" you could be compared against similar businesses much larger than you are, and thus you could pay more in taxes. You should pay the appropriate amount based on what you have.

C. Sales Tax

In order to be exempt from sales tax on merchandise for resale, you will need a tax number. This is issued by your state, and you will need this number not only to participate in certain shows, but you will need this to get into wholesale shows, or at least not be charged sales tax when you go to one. When you buy merchandise tax-free, there is a state requirement that you will resell the goods and collect the sales tax on items sold.

These taxes are usually paid quarterly. If you have lots of sales, you could pay monthly. Most of the time quarterly is the most common timeframe. You will need to pay the money when this is due. You may want to set up a special savings account to separate sales tax dollars, as it is tempting to spend everything you have on inventory and business expenses. Taxes, unfortunately, are another expense.

Here is another word of caution: to qualify for a tax number, you are expected to make a certain amount of money in retail sales. Each state has a different requirement for the minimum dollar amount you are expected to incur. You will need to contact your state's tax payer services office for more information regarding your state. Of course being a new business, achieving this qualifying amount may take a while. If however, over a period of time, you fail to make this amount in sales, your number could be closed. The state officials have deemed that you are costly to keep up! What now, if you don't have a tax number? What if you still sell products through other means where a tax number is not a requisite? Talk to your tax advisor. Even if you do not have a tax number, you still may be required to collect sales tax and submit it to the state. Where I live, I have heard stories about state government officials going to shows, collecting the vendors' social security numbers and names, and giving them an address to which to send tax monies collected! There is also the issue of State and Federal Income Tax on additional money you make. Obviously, the less money you make, the less in taxes you pay, but hey, you are trying to boost sales and money, aren't you? Work your business hard, so your number is valid until you choose not to be in business anymore. Now I have presented to you what I believe to be the top areas you need to address when starting a business.

Cream for Your Coffee?

Your second task is to ask yourself the following questions:

1. Do I have the time to pursue jewelry-making on a higher level?
2. Am I willing to devote time and energy into making a career out of this task?
3. What is my niche market?
4. Am I willing to educate myself on the latest fashion trends, and learn new jewelry-making techniques to help me better my technical skills or expand a product line?
5. Am I willing to network with others?
6. Am I willing to search for good vendor sources?
7. Do I have back-up plans for production of my pieces, in case of illness or order overload?
8. Am I willing to find assistants and train them when needed?
9. Am I willing to market my products?
10. Am I willing to put funds and energy into purchasing fixtures in order to help sell my merchandise?
11. Can I deliver what I promise a buyer?
12. Can I deliver items when scheduled
13. Am I willing to go through the legal steps to comply with business requirements?

These questions should make you start thinking. In the following chapters I will give some further suggestions on how to continue preparing for selling your pieces. These tips will help raise your awareness and help you lay down a foundation for being successful. I know I always try to cover my bases in anything I do so that I am not blind sided. It is my goal to help you follow a path to taking your craft to a higher level. What is just your hobby now can be a profitable and rewarding business in the future!

General Business Information:

Business License Number: _____

Certificate of Resale Number (Tax Number): _____

Effective Date: _____

Tax Preparer: _____

Address: _____

Tel: _____

Tax Attorney: _____

Address: _____

Tel: _____

County Clerk (issues business license): _____

Address: _____

Tel: _____

Tax Payer Services (Sales Tax): _____

Address: _____

Tel: _____

Tax Assessor (Personalty Tax): _____

Address: _____

Tel: _____

List of Questions for Tax Preparer

1. How do I get a business license?

_____

2. How do I get a Sales Tax Number?

_____

3. How often do I have to pay Sales Tax?

_____

4. What do I do if my Tax Number is taken away?

_____

5. What do I do about collecting sales tax if I don't have a Tax Number, but I still sell products?

_____

6. How do I handle gift certificates in relation to sales tax?

_____

7. How do I handle employees and their taxes?

_____

8. How do I do Payroll?

_____

9. How do I calculate percents for FICA, SS, and Worker's Compensation?

_____

10. How often and where do I send payments for FICA, SS, and Worker's Compensation?

_____

11. How do I calculate profits, and what percent is taken out for Federal Income Tax?

_____

12. How do I handle trade-outs/bartered items? Is this ever appropriate to do?

_____

13. Do I have to do inventory at the end of the year?

_____

14. Tell me about Personalty Tax-what is it, how do I figure it out, what counts and does not count when filling out the appropriate forms?

_____

15. How do you recommend I set up an accounting of my business activities-purchases, sales, overhead, etc.?

_____

Vendor Information

Vendor Name	Address	Telephone	Email	Items They Sell
wire-sculpture.com	P.O. Box 1505222 Ogden, UT 84415	1-877-636-0608	customerservice @wire-sculpture.com	Beads, Gemstones, Wire, Tools, DVDs, Swarovki, Cabochons, Patterns, Findings

Chapter Three
100% Fresh Brew: Taking the Plunge

You've thought about it. You've talked about it with your friends and family. You've muddled it over and over in your head, and now you've made the final decision: you're going for it! It's time to take the plunge. Ok, now what? What's the next thing you do when you set up a business, and complete all the necessary paperwork? You look for a work location! Granted, this is probably not going to be a call to a commercial realtor to locate an ideal location, but your house or apartment is a great start. After all, you want to keep overhead low when you are just starting out. Many successful businesses and services began out of someone's living room or garage. As their business grew, they needed to find other means of accommodating this growth. At this time, you are small and getting started, but that still does not negate the fact that you need space in which to work.

Shop Talk: Setting up Your Studio

You will want to find an area in your home where you can work peacefully and without being disturbed. When you are in this space, it is as though you are at another job. A boss would not want workers disturbed, and as you're the boss, you don't want to be disturbed. This means trying to have someone watch the kids; turn off the phone, and definitely no TV! Some light music if you wish but nothing else. This area is called a "studio" and you will birth many things here, such as logos, business names, business cards, fliers, brochures, designs, and jewelry products. You get the idea. This is your sanctum, and it needs to be respected as your time and place to be productive. This is a good thing because you know that you are the ruler here, the head master, and you are in complete control! Sounds nice, doesn't it!

Ok, enough fantasizing; it's time to start setting up. After all, you may be spending lots of time here. Every studio is set up to help the designer with his or her work. You will need a computer, a work table, book shelf, and an assortment of containers to hold wire, rulers, markers, tape, beads, findings, tools, and other items too numerous to mention. You will find the fixtures and other items you need as you go along. Don't forget the office supplies, such as paper, pens, labels, and other materials to help package supplies. You will want to include reference materials such as jewelry books and catalogs for inspiration and notebooks to house vendor or other marketing information. You will want one special notebook to place drawings or cut-outs of jewelry, which will serve as an inspiration book. This will serve you well when you get designer's block and need a jolt to come up with your next project. Good lighting is a must, and magnification accessories are a plus to help prevent fatigue and eye strain. Get a good chair with strong back support so you physically last longer. You want to consider good ergonomics so you don't cause injury to yourself. Learn how to use your tools properly to prevent wrist, arm, and hand strain.

Will That Be Regular or Decaf?
Your Style Choice, Please

Now that you're all cozy in your new workspace, and feeling rather proud (and you should because this is a big step forward), it's time to take a hard look at how you want to use the wire you have, for example. Do you want to create bracelets, rings, necklaces, earrings? You'll want different cuts of wire, such as square, round, half round. Consider hardness, such as full hard, half hard, dead soft; and don't forget to carry different wire gauges, like 22, 24, 18, so you'll have different thickness to use for making components or for simply wrapping. Depending on what you want to create and how to engineer it, you'll need to have the type of wire and associated hardness, cut, and gauge for the projects you'll make. If you like sculpting with wire, you'll need a hardness of dead soft. If you like making bracelets and bangles or wrapping cabochons, you'll want to work with a half hard wire that is square so you can stack and wrap the bundles into a form.

Don't forget that you can also make your own findings and components from wire, such as clasps or ear wires. Coiled wire is a great add-on to your jewelry for a casual, decorative look. If you like a lot of swirls and loops, you might want to add a wire jig to your tool collection. This jig is a board with holes, in which you insert pegs of difference diameters. You can take the wire and wrap around these pegs. Based on the way you insert the pegs, you can come out with some pretty cool designs for earring drops or necklace connectors. You may even want to try your hand at making wire sliders with beads so you can intermingle with some great decorative chain, perhaps. Your work space is a place that is your testing ground and your production area. Don't be afraid to try out new ideas and new styles. If you mess up or something doesn't work out, not a problem! Just try something else or re-work your design. Don't forget to save your bags of scrap wire so they can be sold to a wire company or jeweler. Many companies and some private jewelers are now available to buy scrap metal, and the cash they'll give you allows you to buy new supplies; and it's a great way to recycle. A quick search on the Internet and a few phone calls will help you locate a source that will buy scrap metal for instant cash.

Caffeine Junkies Unite! It's School Time

Most great artists have studied under a master or experienced artisan. Some become greater known than their teachers. I highly recommend that you take some classes in your area that offer techniques you want to learn.

Some of you may be thinking, "But I'm self-taught; I don't need classes!" I say this, "More power to you!" If you have been able to teach yourself good skills, and you are able to sell your jewelry with your own technique and style, that's great! Keep doing what you're doing. For those of you who are not so fortunate, it may be off to school you go!

What are the benefits of classes anyway? For one thing, you get personal hands-on assistance. The teacher can quickly show or explain a technique to you and go at your pace. You are shown a correct way to execute a task so that your piece looks professionally completed. They can explain shortcuts, problem-solving ideas, sizing and measurement tricks, safety issues, as well as discuss different styles and trends. Try different teachers because you will find that you may connect better with a certain personality style. This helps make your learning more rewarding and relaxing. There have been several customers who have stated that they had a frustrating experience with a particular teacher or were uncomfortable in another environment. When they came to my shop, for example, they had a great time in my classroom setting and with the teacher that taught the class. Don't give up when frustration sets in; changing instructors may make all the difference between your producing nothing and your producing a great line to offer potential customers. Last of all, taking a class provides you with the opportunity to meet other students who can share their ideas and experiences, which may in turn help you. This is also a great way to make new friends and network. I've had students in my classes become great friends. Who knows, you might just meet your next business partner!

But what about those whose schedules do not accommodate formal classes, or what if you live in a remote area where they are not readily available? Luckily there are actually some really good DVDs out there that will serve as a great substitute. I recommend DVDs that are made using a two-camera shoot so that you are viewing the teacher over their shoulder. Why is this so important? Many tutorials film using one camera. When you try the techniques yourself, you find that you have to switch everything in your mind to do it correctly. You did not view the instructions as if you were doing it yourself. A DVD that is created with front and rear camera shots allows you to view the techniques process, as you will do them on your own. Wire-Sculpture.com has a tremendous resource of DVDs that are made using two cameras for front and rear views. The teacher in the DVDs is clear, concise, and the close-ups are phenomenal!

Where can you take classes? First, I recommend checking with a local bead shop to see if they offer classes in what you want to learn. Many shops offer wire artistry classes at different levels. There are several bead show circuits offering classes, such as the Bead and Button Show in Milwaukee, WI, or Philadelphia, PA. Beadfest is another circuit that travels, to different states all over the nation. They attract a wide variety of teachers offering a multitude of classes, including wire working. Wire-Sculpture.com also sponsors wire artistry workshops all over the nation. The teachers are top notch, and it will be well worth it to attend one of their sponsored classes. Make a commitment or pilgrimage to further your education if you need to. It will be the smartest move you can make towards your success, and the jewelry you sell will only be a smooth return on your investment.

Don't Be a Drip:
No Copycats Allowed!

This topic of copycats and copyright usually stirs up a hot debate, which I usually try to avoid. However, I feel a need to briefly address it. I am not a copyright attorney, nor do I specialize in this area, so I am not dispensing legal advice. I do want to point out a few things to help create an awareness of this issue because it's bound to come up at one time or another.

There are two camps of thought on this topic. One camp states that you cannot copyright a piece of jewelry, because if a flair or twist is made here or there, then you have a newer style of jewelry that is different from the original. Further thinking suggests that because there are so many similar styles out there it's difficult to determine truly original designs. After all, many minds are found to think alike. The other camp plainly states that copyright infringement is simply illegal, and don't copy someone else's design! One of my teachers is adamant about this. She indicates that when others copy her work and take credit for it, she is robbed of potential income.

Yes, it's true that copyright infringement is illegal, when you are using someone else's design, words, or music score (to name a few areas), without getting permission from the creator or giving appropriate credit. There is, however, the situation of taking a piece that is all ready out there, and re-making another totally unique piece that was inspired by the original. For example, taking a jewelry design and simply changing a bead color, or switching a bead or two, does not make your piece that different. If you do this and try to sell the piece at a show, or submit it to a contest for prize money, you may get a nasty letter or phone call telling you to stop. If you see jewelry that you want to mimic, you will want to design yours so that it is remarkably different.

This means if you were to put the original and yours side by side, you would see two different pieces. If you want to sell or use someone else's design, ask their permission, and do not claim it as your own! At the very least give credit to the person who inspired it and not to yourself. Most artists I have spoken to are more than fine with your making their designs as long as you give them credit. But face it: once you put your designs out there for the public to see, you also stand a chance of being copied.

You either can take it as a form of flattery and that someone actually thinks you're good. Or, you can become angry and try to take the situation to a higher level-that of litigation. From what I have heard, fighting copyright infringement is extremely timely and costly. If a court deems that the other's "copy" of your work is different enough, then you may be out of luck and lots of money. If you continue to feel the desire to copyright your design, you can go through this process by contacting the US Copyright Office.

Enough on copyright! But I do want to talk a little more about inspiration and design. I keep magazines and other pictures of designs on hand for sources of inspiration. That's usually how new things evolve. Check out fashion magazines and jewelry catalogs. Take a trip to some local boutiques in your area and look closely at what's on the racks. These sources are great for inspiration and a means of kicking off your creativity. But as a designer you want to make pieces that are truly yours. That's what being a designer is—one who creates and strives to put out fun and unique items. Taking what "is" to a different level.

Designer Set-up Checklist

1. Where will my workspace be located?

_____

2. What time will I choose to be my regular "Hours of Operation?"

_____

3. If I have Internet access, what will my business account email address be? (Internet companies usually let an account holder set up several email addresses. You may want to set up one identifying your business email – e.g. greatdesigner@provider.com)

_____

Shop Items Checklist: (to get you started!)

Item	Obtained (Y/N)
Work Table	
Seating	
Lighting	
Magnification	
Tools (Pliers, Cutters, etc.)	
Tool Holder	
Design Board	
Color Wheel	
Storage containers	
Measuring Tape/Ruler	
Measurement gauges (rings, etc.)	
Jewelry Displays	
Bookshelf	
Inspirational Sources	
Computer	
Printer	
Price Tags/Labels	
Pens/Pencils	

Niche Markets

Write down the market areas in your community where you can provide products reflecting their venue. (Some examples include bridal, pet, etc.) This will change as you change your avenues or style. You may find new areas to create and market products later in your career.

1._____
2._____
3._____
4._____
5._____
6._____
7._____
8._____
9._____
10._____

Classes I Have Taken:

1. _____
2. _____
3. _____
4. _____
5. _____
6. _____
7. _____
8. _____
9. _____
10. _____

Classes I Want To Take:

1. _____
2. _____
3. _____
4. _____
5. _____
6. _____
7. _____
8. _____
9. _____
10. _____

DVDs/Wire Books/Wire Magazines

1. _____
2. _____
3. _____
4. _____
5. _____
6. _____
7. _____
8. _____
9. _____
10. _____

Wire Instruction Websites

1. *wire-sculpture.com* _____
2. _____
3. _____
4. _____
5. _____
6. _____
7. _____
8. _____
9. _____
10. _____

Chapter Four
Mellow, Mild, or Nutty? Creating Your Line

It's time to get down to brass tacks—creating that line you've been dreaming about. Determining your niche or area on which you want to focus will be the springboard for starting a line. After all, you are setting up some special products reflecting this market and the income of the buyers associated with it. A jewelry line commanding higher price points may have designs that are more intricate in their construction, may contain higher grades of materials, and will cater to that buyer who has expendable income.

An artisan in my town has her jewelry boutique located in a high-tourist area. She carries a variety of earrings, necklaces, and bracelets. Her merchandise reflects high grade gemstones, precious metals, and quality craftsmanship. Her prices range from the upper double digits to over a thousand dollars! Needless to say, her buyer will be someone who has the extra money and desire for a specialty piece. Most of the jewelry in her cases is not just for fancy social occasions, either. She is catering to a high-end market, perhaps a tourist passing through who wants a fine necklace to commemorate a memorable vacation. She has locals who know her work and buy an occasional piece. She has determined her market and niche. I spoke to a lady one day who indicated that she had done very well at a local church expo held one weekend. Asked how she fared in her sales, she proudly announced that she had done quite well, but that her pieces were affordable. She added that she catered to the moderate-income market because someone needs to cater to them, too! I had to smile because she clearly knew her market, jewelry type, and price points.

Have you decided what your line will contain? Do you want to represent a variety of jewelry types – ring, bracelets, and earrings? Do you want to focus on more dressy jewelry or casual pieces that can be worn most anytime? When I look at the booths at the artisan craft shows we have yearly, I see some with only one focus, such as wire crafted pieces. Others I see may have items fashioned by metalsmithing and focus on perhaps an animal theme. Then there are those who choose to create several types of items hoping to have something for everyone. All good choices, when presented well.

You will have to decide if you want to be focused with a special theme or be eclectic with a variety of styles. Some people like making just earrings, which tend to be a popular item at shows, followed by bracelets. These items are simple to make, can have affordable price points, and many buyers like to wear them on a regular basis. It's just easy to spring for a pair of fun earrings or a trendy bangle. That's not to say necklaces and pins don't have their place, because I see gorgeous ones all the time; and they sell well. You will have to make a choice in what you want to present to the public. A theme usually creates a focus for the buyer where they can view choices that reflect an artist's style and expertise. The theme creates momentum as items are viewed and in the end creates an interest and desire to buy. If eclectic is over-done by too many different styles represented, a buyer becomes confused, overwhelmed, and may walk away, as nothing stands out and draws them in.

Yesterday's Choice

I am a lover of antiques and vintage period items, whether it be furniture, clothing, or other collectibles. Jewelry is definitely my favorite category. There are all kinds of books out in the market place showing beautiful and detailed pictures of jewelry from the Victorian, Art Nouveau, and Art Deco Periods. You will also find books on vintage jewelry dating back to the '30s. The best part about the earlier periods of jewelry is the fact that the designs are copyright-free! These eras boast beautiful and distinct styles that are still sought after and loved today. Also, re-creation of these pieces rendered in wire and beads is fun, and your jewelry will be totally unique! If you are keener on the Victorian look, why not create gorgeous lavalieres, and pretty pendant necklaces? Earrings are another category, sporting curves and dangles, not unlike the chandelier pieces of today. Art Deco will require more geometric lines and straighter looks that create a clean presentation. Art Nouveau could pose a little more challenging task, due to the floral nature and curvature involved in the design, but this will only bring out the creative instinct in you. Design books showing jewelry from each time period can give you ideas from which to choose. Period pieces are definitely worth considering if you want a line that brings the past into the present.

That Signature Flavor

Have you ever seen a particular style of art and knew just by looking at it who the creator was? Thomas Kinkade paintings are characterized by the use of color to create the effects of glowing lights. The Elsa Peretti line sold at Tiffany & Company shows sleek smooth curvature. Heavy patterning and bright faceted gemstones are highly characteristic of David Yurman and John Hardy pieces. You may want to consider adding that little something extra to your pieces. Your signature style may be including a rosette or curly swirl to all of your designs. You may simply choose to have a jewelry tag made where you can stamp your business name or motif on to a tiny plate and attach this to each piece. Microstamp is a company who fashions small die stamps with your logo. You can then place this die on a blank tag, which they also sell, and merely with one stroke of a hammer have your tag ready to use. This is a great way to add your name to each item you make. Tiffany does this; you can too!

What's My Line?

1. What type of jewelry do I want to create? (e.g. Bracelets, Earrings)

_____

2. What will be my signature?

_____

3. How will I obtain my signature?

_____

4. What price buyer type do I want? __High __Medium __Low

5. What price points do I want?

_____

6. Do I want a theme (animal, flowers, etc.), or do I want eclectic?

_____

7. Do I want dressy or everyday-wear type jewelry?

_____

8. What material(s) will I work with? (e.g. Wire, Glass, Gemstones)

_____

9. Do I like period styles? If so, which one?

_____

10. How is the period style of my choice fashioned?

_____

Chapter Five
Getting Down to the Grind: Pricing, Somebody's Gotta Do It!

This is probably the least favorite and hardest part of doing business. Everyone will tell you that they have a hard time trying to figure out how to price their jewelry. Unfortunately, this is part of the job, and I haven't found that magic genie in the bottle that will just zap everything out there for you. It does take work.

First of all, there is a difference between just wanting to get your money back for what you paid in supplies versus actually making a profit sufficient enough to support the operations of a business and pay yourself. The first level of thinking is called supporting my hobby. There is nothing wrong with this if you are doing this on a light level, and you are not concerned with making a large profit. If you want to actually make money to support a business and pay yourself, you are going to have to charge more than just what you put into materials. There are others who have presented some formulas on how to price your jewelry. Though they allow you to make a profit if you follow the outlines, taking the time to determine the base numbers and doing the math is a little daunting. To follow these formulas, you need to know your overhead expenses, production time, production output amounts, and desired wages. If you work in spurts, some of these areas can be tricky to calculate, and you also begin to find that some of these numbers are truly arbitrary based on your personal choices or needs. Though there will be some initial decision-making that will be required for any method you chose, there are quicker ways for determining price so that the above-mentioned areas are accounted for. I'll note a few of them for you.

Cost of Goods Times Desired Markup

The simplest means of determining a price is by merely taking your cost of goods and multiplying by a chosen number that reflects your desired markup. When I made bridal jewelry to sell, I priced goods this way, taking my materials cost and multiplying by 5. A necklace that cost me $7.00 to make ended up wholesaling for $35.00. (Cost of materials - $7.00 x 5 = $35.00) A teacher I know also suggests this as a good simple method if you are a hobbyist or crafter. She also recommends a variation on this by multiplying cost of goods x 3, plus $10/hour, if you're proficient at what you do. These methods are good especially for wire artistry and metal clay pieces. In general the markup you do covers everything involved in creating the piece, including labor.

Pricing Software

You can also use a jewelry pricing program if you wish. There are a few different packages available on the market and with various price tags. Search terms online like "jewelry pricing," "jewelry inventory tracking," or "jewelry inventory management," just to name a few. You will need to know this information for tax purposes, and one of these programs will save you time in obtaining that information when you need it. These programs allow you to input your inventory, manage stock levels, price your jewelry, track orders, and pull reports with specific information that you want to know. Each system will have some of their own unique features, so you will have to determine what will fit your personal needs and budget. There is one drawback to all of these products (as with any pricing software or accounting package): you do have to engage in the administrative work of entering your inventory parts. Again, there is no magic genie to zap the information into the program for you, but perhaps a good administrative assistant may be helpful at a later time. In the meantime, you will have to do this yourself.

Volume Discounting

Volume discounting is not uncommon. Though you don't have to offer this, it does encourage increased spending, because your buyer appreciates the deal they are getting, and their savings may spur them on to buy more from you. You make a business decision where you want your cut-offs to be in relation to percentages off. For example, you may choose to offer a 15% discount for orders over $150; 20% for purchases over $200; 25% for purchases greater than $500.

Other Pricing Caveats

There are some things to consider when choosing a markup for pricing or creating your labor schedule, should you choose the method I just described. First you will need to consider the income of your clientele. More modest income clients will not pay higher prices like a clientele with more expendable income. You will either need to consider the cost of materials used or create pieces that do not require much labor for the task involved. Also consider the region in which you live. It is a known fact that clients from certain regions of the country will pay higher prices, while those in other regions would never dream of paying the prices you ask. The last issue pertains to determining labor costs. Unfortunately, I hear beaders lament constantly that clients don't want to pay for labor. I have discovered that unless the client truly understands and appreciates the time and effort to construct a piece, the piece itself only has a perceived value when viewed upon completion. This means that unless you are in the right market, it is sometimes hard to get $400 for that woven piece that took you two weeks to make. I know artists who receive such prices, but they are able to break into a market that will bear it. This doesn't mean that you shouldn't charge for labor – you just may need to consider your product line and the time it takes to create it. At worst, you may actually have to look at your labor costs and adjust accordingly.

Last of all, you may want to check your local department stores for a reality check on what jewelry items cost. Just because the Calvin Klein® and Monet items are commanding $48 price tags for a bracelet doesn't necessarily mean you can too. Some people believe (erroneously) that brand-name, store-bought goods are just better, and they may pay the price; some people just go for the item because it's a brand. The other truth is that many wait for a good sale. It all boils down to how customers view hand-crafted jewelry versus machine cast pieces. You will need to educate your buyers regarding the materials that make up pieces and the time it takes you to complete them. In this way they become more informed consumers who, hopefully, will see that a hand-crafted piece of jewelry is more special than a department store brand.

Pricing Sheet

There are several ways to price your designs. Listed below are a few simpler ways to do this.

Materials Pricing

Cost of Materials: _____ x 5 = _____

Cost of Materials x 3 = _____ + $10/hr = _____

Labor Pricing/Repair Schedule

Stringing: Single Strand $_____/in.

$_____ for crimp & clasp

Multiple Strands

1st Strand $_____/in; Crimp: $_____

2nd Strand $_____/in.; Crimp $_____

3rd Strand $_____/in.; Crimp $_____

4th Strand and up $_____/in.; Crimp $_____

Pearl/Gemstone Knotting

$_____/in.

$_____ for knot covers & clasp

$_____ for French wire & clasp

Tin Cup Style

$_____/section

$_____ for knot covers/end cones & clasp

$_____ for crimping & clasp

Earrings/Linked Items

$_____ /pair (earrings) for *simple* loop

$_____ for *simple* loop thereafter

$_____ /pair (earrings) for *wired (coiled)* loop

$_____ /*wired (coiled)* loop thereafter

Chain: $_____ /pair + each loop or coil

Design Fee

$_____ / Project (dollars per project)

Use this fee when you are custom-designing or re-designing an item for a customer. You spend time in creating their piece, and you should be compensated for your time and effort.

Notes on Fee Schedule

This schedule does not include the cost of materials. You will need to determine that amount and include with your labor costs noted in this schedule. Determine what is appropriate for your market. You may want to collect 50% of the payment up front from the customer, with the remainder to be paid at pick-up time.

Allow a 30-90 day retrieval time frame, after which time, the item becomes your property, or can be sold. Let the customer know your policies up front so they can make an informed decision on how to proceed. A signed contract is best so that all parties know what is expected. The contract should include any designs agreed upon, specifics surrounding this design, labor involved, and completion and pick-up times.

Chapter Six
The Writing's On the Bag: Marketing Materials

No business is complete without marketing materials. You will definitely need to provide a way for your customers to contact you in the future should they request your merchandise or services. If you are marketing to high-end galleries and boutiques, you will want to share the following information:

1. A description of yourself as the artist
2. Your style of work
3. Pictures of your work
4. Prices of products.

When working with shops where you are asked to present several choices for customers, you may need to construct a catalog showing the styles you offer. These are just a few examples of what you will need to address when creating marketing materials. Before I go into more detail about specific marketing items, let me share a few observations. Some will agree wholeheartedly with me, and some may disagree, but here I go anyway!

First of all, marketing materials can be expensive to produce depending on which company you use to produce them, materials you use, and to what extent you maximize the space on your material of choice. The sad thing I have found from experience and personal observation is that no matter how expensive or "Wow!" the business card or brochure, I did not necessarily find an increase in my business after handing them out. Nor have I heard anyone personally tell me that just handing out their expensive business cards brought them more revenue than those who printed their cards from a home computer. I have had the glossy brochures with the professional photography and copy. I have had gorgeous business cards on deluxe parchment or incredible vinyl. Guess what—they still got lost, misplaced, or worse yet, trashed. Most of all, business did not increase.

Does this mean that having marketing materials is a big waste of time, so don't bother? Absolutely not! Being the paper nut that I am, I'll go to just about any length I can afford to have a cutting edge look or cool card for someone to remember me by. I appreciate receiving a really nice card or neat brochure. However, I too, end up throwing them in the trash at some point, after I've spent a brief time admiring them. I do keep the cards from vendors and people I want to contact again or with whom I do business on a regular basis, regardless of how the card looks. My cousin, who made a great living in the marketing industry, told me years ago that he knew of colleagues who carried two types of business cards—cheaper versions to hand out to the general public, so they could have contact information, and a more expensive vinyl card saved for those clients who specifically conducted business with them on a regular basis. Carrying doubles of something may be stretching it a bit for you at this point, and the cost would not be worth it. Nor will it be worth the cost to invest in fancy over-the-top stocks such as vinyl and other plastic grades.

There are cheaper alternatives which can be used to produce your materials, such as using your own computer. Card and paper stock, quality printers and inks that are now available have made it possible for you to create products on demand and at a more reasonable cost. There are cute clipart logos you can use, and many are available for free. If you use one of these logos from the Internet, make sure there are no stipulations for commercial use. Copy centers such as FedEx Kinkos, Staples, and other office supply stores provide printing services, and can help you create eye-catching cards, brochures, or press kits. If you want to create a logo and a look that is truly yours and reflects better what you do, consider looking for a graphic arts student who may need a client for a school project and would post you on his or her own website as a customer they have assisted. This would be free advertising for you! They can create an image that can be used for letterhead, business cards, and even a website. What exactly are some of the specific things you need for marketing yourself and letting others know you are out there? Below are listed some of the standard items. You may have to create some different ones to fit your customers' needs as you increase your business.

Branding Yourself: Business Cards

These are tried and true and the most common means of informing people about your business. Carry them at all times! These cards are small, easily tucked away in a wallet or special card file. You can include fun logos reflecting your business name, have a nice photo of a showstopper piece you've created, not to mention your name and other contact information, such as address, phone number, website, and email address. The nice thing, too, is that you can also create double-sided cards so you can increase your mileage on advertising your business and including some highlighted information in just a small amount of space. As suggested earlier, these cards can be glossy looking, printed on vellum for a parchment feel, or actually printed on a plastic material called vinyl. You can even obtain business cards that are truly plastic like credit cards (do this only if you want to spend an incredible amount of money!) For a more affordable choice, you can also create cards on nice simple card stock purchased from an office supply store and print them from your computer. There are also online websites that provide templates for you to upload images and include the typed copy you wish to have printed on the cards. When you complete the template, you can submit the image and the company will print the number of cards you request. How convenient is that? Usually the more unique looking and eye-catching the card, the more people may be inclined to hang on to it, especially if they are very interested in what you do and wish to contact you later.

Take It Up a Notch: Post Cards

Another fun way of promoting your business is through the use of post cards. Though this cannot be stored as discreetly as a business card, a post card is good to place on your table when you are doing a show, and it can also be mailed as an advertisement or invitation to a show or party you may be having. The size of the card allows for a broader spectrum of information to be shared. You can also place maps and other directions as well as good pictures of items you may be introducing. Post cards are usually created on heavier paper known as card stock, which comes in all kinds of textures and colors. Post cards can also be created on your home computer or you can hire a company to print them for you. These tend to be more costly due to size and double-sided printing.

Full Steam Ahead!: Brochures

This marketing tool is a nice way of allowing yourself an opportunity to go into more detail about your business, including you as the artist, and the products you produce. The panels that make up the brochure allow you to create nice sections where you can share more specific information devoted to a selected subject of your choice. For example, the front panel, which is the first area seen by a viewer, will usually show the name of your business, your logo, and some brief contact information. Your inner panels are usually divided into two or three sections, depending on your preference for a single-fold, or double-fold brochure style. You can further subdivide these sections to cover more information you wish to share. For example, in a single fold style, the first inner panel may describe you as the artist, and even contain a picture of you. You may describe your jewelry line in the second panel, outlining product types (bracelets, necklaces, and earrings), materials used, and finally including some small pictures of some of your pieces. The back of the brochure (the outside panel) is usually blank so you can print addresses of customers for mailing. Brochures can also be designed and printed on your computer. Microsoft Publisher is one of many software packages on the market, which allows you to formulate different publishing projects to meet your needs. You select a template style and make changes in copy or graphics as needed. Once you have your project completed, you may either print multiple copies from your own computer or take a copy to a local printer for larger quantities.

Coffee Klatch: Press Kit

You hear of people talking about press kits. What are these anyway? Press kits act as your resume, so to speak. A kit contains a collection of information about your business, such as the following:

1. Your artist's biography
2. A review of your company and the products you offer
3. Pictures of your "star" or signature pieces
4. A copy of any newsletters you send out

5. Press releases you may have had
6. Awards you may have achieved
7. Companies that sell your lines

This information is usually housed in a nice presentation folder, which should also include your business card and contact information. If you have a website, printed page excerpts from this would be nice to include. Usually press kits are given to those customers who are more serious about carrying your work and wish to have more complete information about you and what you do. These are not given out to the casual buyer, as it would be information overload. Usually high end galleries and upscale boutiques will want a press kit so they have a good familiarity with who you are and what you can provide to them and their customers. If you ever decide to teach your craft, educational settings will want more information about your skills and competence level regarding your craft. Again, if you do the press kits yourself, you can address the contents more affordably using your own computer and some nice paper and card stock, as well as a quality printer. Keep a few packets of these available so that you will be prepared to sell yourself to a prospective buyer at any time. It's much easier to be prepared with this material rather than try to frantically pull something together at a moment's notice. You will look more professional, prepared, and serious about your business.

Brand Listings: Catalog

Catalogs are very useful to provide pricing for your different buyer types, such as wholesale, retail, or consignment. I usually reserve catalogs for those customers that are buying my products in quantity amounts. These should not ordinarily be handed out to the casual buyer at a show, for example. When I worked with bridal shops in town, I created a picture catalog which included a picture of the jewelry piece, a brief description, and the retail price. I did not include the wholesale price directly on this catalog. That price went on another pricing sheet. This was done so the customer would not know wholesale pricing; yet, they could still be able to select a jewelry style and type they wanted, such as a necklace or pair of earrings.

From Our House to Yours: CD

If you really want to keep up with today's technology, you can put your information on a CD. With a CD you can make your information more detailed, such as including a slide show of your product line. You can create Word documents outlining your artist's biography, price catalogs with pictures, and a host of information you wish to share. The nice thing about the CD is that the recipient can copy these files directly to their personal computer and can readily pull up your information whenever they wish. If you want to be unique in your presentation style, this might be a way to go. Regardless of the materials you create, make sure that they are nicely written, are free of typographical errors, and clearly state what you can do for the customer. Clear and concise images are a focus for any of your marketing materials. With the host of digital cameras on the market today, you may be able to make your own pictures, using natural outdoor lighting for best results. If you don't trust your abilities as a photographer, you may want to hire one to assist you. Professional pictures will enhance your look as well as help get your work included in a juried show. A bad picture can be a major pitfall. Most importantly of all, carry business cards with you at all times, and determine the other materials you will need as your business grows.

Marketing Materials

Determine the marketing materials you need for your business. You will expand these as you grow.

Business Cards (check those choices you like)

Single Sided	
Double Sided	
Block Type	
Script Type	
Other Type	
Glossy	
Matte	
Vellum/Parchment	
Vinyl	
Plastic	
Logo (select at print shop)	
Logo (use your own)	
Include a Picture of Your Work	
Number of Cards	
Notes:	

Brochures

Single Fold	
Double Fold	
Section Subjects	
Font	
Inclusion of Pictures	
Notes:	

Press Kit Check List

Nice Pocket Folder	
Cover Letter Outlining Kit Contents	
Brochure (if you have one)	
Bio of You the Artist	
Company History & Other Interesting Facts About You or Your Company	
Company Ideas/Mission Statement	
Company Goals	
Product Line Description	
Services Offered	
Copies of Press Releases Copy of Company Newsletter	
Copies of Magazine Articles About Your Company	
Pictures of Your Work	
Listing of Events You Attend	
List of Retail Locations	
Business Card Inserted in Folder	
Notes:	

Use nice folders, paper and card stock when putting a press kit together. You are creating a first impression and you want to look professional. In your folder start off with your cover letter and then you can list the items in the order presented above. Make sure bios and other information are clearly printed using a computer and nice quality stock paper. Ensure that the font is clear and legible. Avoid certain script fonts which prove difficult to read. Keep copies of press kits on hand to be delivered to appropriate parties when opportunities arise. These should be reserved for serious buyers, who may be requesting your services or items on a regular basis.

Chapter Seven
Java Jolt!
Ideas on Where to Sell Your Jewelry

When you determined your niche, you already had some ideas about your market. You may have created your line around the style and likely preferences for people in that market. Color choice and other signature motifs most likely were included to make the pieces more specialized and unique. Bridal and formal jewelry will have a completely different look than sorority jewelry, or casual daily wear pieces that can be worn to the office. Each of these types serves a different customer base. The good news for you is that your market place is huge! I'll tell you why.

One year I participated in a show that was designed just for women. Owning a bead shop, I thought there would be lots of people who would like to learn to make their own jewelry. Well, was I way off. Oh, there were some that were interested, but I found out that most people just want to buy ready-made items. That means that you won't be competing with the concept of people wishing to craft their own designs. This gives you and edge on selling your pieces to a wide marketplace. If you have created some eclectic and everyday-wear jewelry, there are a number of places where you could sell to a variety of customers. Below I will outline some of these avenues, which are niche markets as well. Please consider this listing as merely brainstorming. You may have other ideas that I may have either overlooked or simply have not considered due to unfamiliarity with a certain group or organization. Ready, let's go!

Craft Shows

Craft shows are the most prevalent, and they are found all around the country. They come in a variety of levels from inclusion of the general craftsperson to highly juried shows, where only the most skilled and unique craftsperson is invited to participate. You will need to fill out an application to be accepted into an artisan craft show, and for those shows that are juried you may be selected based on pictures you submit of your work. Juried shows have a selection process carried out by a committee of people, usually other artisans, who review the work of inquiring parties to determine if they have products of a caliber and uniqueness befitting the show that is being produced.

If you are required to submit pictures for jury review, I would recommend you solicit the assistance of a professional photographer. It will be imperative that the lighting, positioning, and display of your select pieces are impeccable. Dark, blurry, and unflattering pictures will destroy your chances of being selected for the show. Don't take chances unless you are a professional photographer yourself! You will need the money to cover booth rent, which can be hundreds of dollars a day or for a block of days. Booth setup is also a consideration, as you will need a tent or pavilion to house your work if the show is outdoors. You will want to make sure that the tent you use can be anchored into the ground and has a roof and walls that can shelter you and your items from the elements, such as the blazing hot sun, or pouring rain. This can also cost some money initially, but you will have it for future shows. Don't forget to consider money for displays, and you may want a mirror so people can see how they look in their new prospective piece. Price points for these events can vary greatly, depending on the buyer to which you are catering. I've seen items that are priced like department stores, to items that are hundreds of dollars. The decision is yours!

Church, School, Community Craft Shows

If you want something a little less stressful for your first time selling, this is the setup I would choose. Usually these events are cheaper in booth rent, and many of them are in-doors in a cafeteria, gym, or hallway setting. The environment is more casual and relaxed. Your setup may include merely a table for placing your items. You will still want displays and good lighting. Price points may need to be more "affordable" to encourage buying, as shows such as these are very family oriented, high-ticket items are not usually expected here. These events are great ones in which to experiment to see what types of jewelry sells the best and to become accustomed to waiting on customers. You will also learn how to write up purchase tickets and handle money. After experiencing a show such as this, you may get a good feel for determining if you like shows or not. Each one is different and has a different customer base. Like most shows, these private, community events also have elements in common with the larger events, such as setup, display, customer service, and handling money.

Galleries

If you believe your work is unique enough, and at a level of craftsmanship to show high quality, you may want to consider seeking out a local artisan gallery that will be willing to carry your jewelry designs. Many galleries are interested in finding new designers, and you could be the one they are looking for! This is where your press kit would come in handy, as it will give the potential gallery owner a review of your product line as well as information about you the artist. You will want to scout out the galleries in your area and see what is being sold. Some are just for glass; some are for artwork, such as paintings, and then there are those that have a mix of artistic mediums. If you see a shop that really strikes your fancy, but you don't see jewelry, you may want to ask the owner if they have ever considered carrying a jewelry line. It never hurts to be the only jewelry exhibitor in the gallery. At least you would have no other competition in this area for the present.

Hotels

When I heard that someone had connected with the hotels in her area, I was impressed. This was definitely an area I had never considered. There are hotel gift shops that could carry some of your jewelry line. However, this lady had an arrangement where she would set up her booth during a convention or other events held at the hotel, and she would sell her jewelry to the attendees during their seminar breaks. She actually did quite well. If there are some big hotels in your area, you may want to approach the manager and inquire if it would be possible to set up a booth in a certain location when there are special events being held at that hotel. You will need to agree upon the following: booth fees or sales percentage, set-up location, and listing of events. You may also want to determine the type of event in case you wish to create jewelry that is suitable for that particular group of attendees. This venue could prove to be profitable, not to mention an exciting way of meeting people and networking. One word of caution: many large corporate hotels do not allow individual business to sell in their establishments. They usually have their own shops and associated buyers who select merchandise for them. If you can't sell in the hotel itself, do consider contacting a buyer to see if your line will work in one of the shops.

Office Parks

What lady wouldn't be pleasantly surprised and thrilled about seeing a table of jewelry for sale in the building as she exits the elevator on her way to lunch? Most of them, I imagine! Women love to buy, and your table would be convenient as people left or entered the building. Each office park is different. The building may be owned by the company itself, or the park may have different businesses which include a general building or property manager who merely addresses property issues. Either way, you will need to determine who the appropriate person is and contact them to see if you could set up in their lobby during lunch hour or for a prescribed amount of time. You will also need to agree upon any fees for set-up or percentage of sales that may need to go to the appropriate party. You may want to try and settle on a scheduled time and date if you would like to sell there on a regular basis.

Individual Businesses

When I was in my last corporate job, our head director was thoughtful enough to allow some Mary Kay representatives to set up in a spare meeting room during the holidays, and give the women in the department an opportunity to shop for gifts. This may be something you could do as well. Why not contact individual businesses and seek permission to set up during a holiday such as Christmas or Valentine's Day? This would give the workers a chance to shop without having to spend a long time away from the office. You will need to speak to a department head or director to do this, and they may be quite open to it. You may also wish to speak to Human Resource departments and offer to create employee appreciation gifts, or items commemorating Breast Cancer Awareness, and/or other "Awareness" issues. You will most likely need a business license to carry out this task since they will need to note this on their books for a tax write-off. Therefore, they will need to note you as a legitimate business vendor. Selling in this manner makes you actually glad you are in the board room!

Shops

Shops can include a variety of choices: boutiques, antique malls, and even other jewelry shops. One lady I know actually started her handcrafted jewelry business by setting up in a corner of a local jeweler's shop. She carried a style that he did not sell: beaded gemstone necklaces, bracelets, and earrings. Boutiques are a wonderful outlet. If an owner is interested in your pieces, you may want to ask if you can match your jewelry with the clothing that is presently on the mannequins, or design a new category style that is being requested by customers. Matching jewelry to clothing can be tricky, especially when working with colors and style, but it's a fun, challenging, and rewarding task. Last of all, antique malls are a potential source for selling your work. Many malls do not require that all your merchandise be totally vintage or antique, but you will need to check with the rules of the mall. You may want to make the jewelry look more vintage-like, or perhaps try to mimic a particular era such as Victorian or Art Deco.

Showrooms

I have a friend who used to scour the marketplace showrooms to see if there was one that would accept her linen line. She was successful in locating one who was willing to include her work with other products in the showroom. Therefore, you may consider trying to find a wholesale showroom where you can include your line with others that are present. These rooms have representatives (reps) that go out to seek buyers for the different lines, which can also include yours. Some drawbacks are the time-consuming task of finding the appropriate showroom and considering bulk volume orders from buyers. This can put you at a potential risk for production over-load. However, this is a possible option depending on what you produce.

Bridal

The wedding industry can be fun and offer several options within it. Designing for the bride is one level, and then there are the other participants, such as bridesmaids, flower girl, and mother-of-the bride. A good way to break into this niche is to find out from the bridal shop owners if they would be interested in a new hand-crafted bridal jewelry line. The bridal shops are the first place a bride will come to select her gown, and she may be in the market for accessories to go with it. You may also contact wedding planners, who can assist in marketing your pieces. After all, they are assisting the brides with everything from church and reception planning, to the wedding cake and other accessories. They can put the word out regarding your jewelry, or better yet, show some samples, if you are inclined to leave some of your designs with them for show.

Another good source is wedding stationery shops or specialists in this arena. Sometimes they carry products other than the traditional invitations and congratulatory cards. If there are wedding shows in your area, you may wish to set up at one of these events. The drawback is that they are usually for one day only, and booth rent can be several hundred dollars. Also, brides may be coming to look and not necessarily buy during these shows. However, if you don't try, you will never know. It will at least provide you with a means of networking and perhaps meeting others who can help get your name out there!

Hospital/Church Gift Shops

Gift shops are another great avenue for selling jewelry. If you go the church route, you can create rosaries, for Confirmation or First Communion. Bracelets for these occasions are also a nice item to add. If you are open to this idea, prayer beads made of gemstones is another great idea that can be created for other faiths, and not just those of Christian origin. If you select hospital gift shops, you may want to consider badge or eyeglass holders for the working professional.

Lanyards are popular today, since many companies require their employees to have ID on them at all times. Fun key chains or zipper pulls may be add-on items for a casual buyer looking for a neat gift for someone. You will need to speak with the buyers for both of these venue types to determine if they would like to have your line in their shops. Price points will need to be considered here as you may be addressing a more moderate income market.

Sororities

Sorority houses or the Pan-Hellenic Buildings on college campuses may offer a great way to advertise your jewelry, especially if you can create wonderful bracelets and necklaces bearing that sorority's colors and Greek letters. Being in the Greek system myself when I was in college, I bought all kinds of items with my sorority letters and colors. If a vendor had come to our suite to show jewelry that I could wear to indicate my sorority membership, I definitely would have bought something.

You may need to approach the person in charge of the Pan-Hellenic building where the sorority suites are housed. At least they will be able to direct you to the correct channels if they are not the decision-maker. If your area colleges have sorority houses instead of suites, you will need to approach the college administration department for permission to contact the house residents. Overall, you may find the Greek System to be very lucrative.

Home Parties

The cosmetics and kitchenware industries have used this form of marketing and selling for decades. You presently do hear of some jewelry brands using home parties as a means for selling their product, such as Cookie Lee and Premiere Designs. Usually the designer has a friend or coworker set up a party, inviting her friends to review the jewelry with the option of purchasing what is on display or ordering based on the display as samples. The hostess of the party may receive jewelry based on the total sales for the evening. If one of the friends of the hostess decides to schedule a party, then the hostess can also receive more in jewelry. These are fun incentives for those choosing to host a party for you. The other benefit is that you keep lots of your profit due to not having booth fees. All you're out is your time and fuel for getting to the hostess's home. Some of my customers have made several hundred dollars in one evening from selling their designs. You will, however, have to continually be looking for people who are willing to set up parties for you. You can also set these up yourself and have people come over to your place. This system will take more active marketing because you will have to continually find people to sponsor the parties.

Dance Clubs

Until I got into ballroom dancing a few years ago, I had never considered this group as one that would be marketable. Females in this arena are dressing up to dance at the studio clubs and may appreciate some fun glitzy pieces to go with their outfits. Ballet and other modern dance groups are target markets as well. Middle Eastern dance, such as belly dancing, is becoming more popular, and there can be some room for creativity regarding waist decorations or large link chain belts holding coin pendants. Price points will be different when catering to adults versus children, but any of these markets can be fun and bring out your creative side.

Sports Teams

You can approach this area from different levels, such as high school, college, or professional. In my area we have several popular college teams as well as a professional team where fan jewelry can be created so you can cheer in style. Don't forget the cheerleaders because you could create some fun jewelry for cheerleading teams. If you choose to go the professional route, you will need to contact someone that heads the marketing department and see if you can set up a table outside the field area during game times. You will also need a vendor's license in order to sell your products. A call to your local county clerk or taxpayer services office may be in order so you will have the paperwork you need as well as a means of submitting any sales tax collected during the event.

Pets

As you may well notice, people love their pets. Dogs especially aren't too opposed to wearing fun, fancy collars for just a short while. Cats may be another matter, though I have a friend who was known for dolling up her cats in bonnets and jewelry. She then placed them in decorative miniature carriages, where they rested peacefully and posed to have their picture taken. You can either embellish the woven nylon collars you see in the pet shops by creating a jeweled drop to hang from the collar ring or buckle end, or you can string a collar made of fun gemstones and crystals. If you want to take this a step farther, you could create a wire collar bangle with a drop coming off the clasp. With businesses such as the doggie daycares popping up everywhere, why not approach one of them to see if they would like to sell your pieces to their animal-loving customers? Grooming centers, kennels, vet offices, and pet boarding centers are also good places for pet jewelry outlets. You can create fun bracelets and necklaces for owners bearing the image of certain dog breeds and cats. If there is a Cat or Dog Fancier Show that comes to your town, you may inquire about setting up a booth. Turn those dog days into profit days!

Baby & Children

When looking for a gift for the newborn, a tiny baby bracelet can be impossible to find since most items are for older children. These are very tiny, fitting around the thumb of an adult male! If you create these, owners of baby and children shops may be only too happy to have this as part of their merchandise. Of course, mothers and grandmothers love to spend money on their little girls or granddaughters by purchasing them a charming necklace or bracelet with a tiny sterling puffed heart or a Swarovski butterfly. Hospital or church gift shops may also like to carry these items for gifts for the newborn or christenings. Possibilities are endless, and you can have some fun with this niche as well.

Holistic & Wellness Fairs

In my area we have a health and wellness fair featuring holistic healing vendors and wellness consultants. At these fairs, you can purchase books, learn about therapies for assisting with mental and physical issues, as well as purchase jewelry. Some items for this arena include chakra bracelets and power and affirmation jewelry. Many gemstones are noted to have healing properties, and jewelry consisting of certain stones can remind the wearer of the benefits of wearing these gemstones. Another item of interest would be the creation of pendulums for divination. You can make gorgeous ones out of gemstone nuggets or larger beads and attach a nice Bali end cone for the point. If you have any metaphysical shops in your community, speak with the appropriate person about carrying your new line of items. Set up a booth at one of the wellness fairs. It's also a great way to meet new contacts, who also may want to carry your jewelry as part of their booth, especially if they travel different circuits.

Calorie Counters

Like the bracelet that inspired me, you can create calorie counters for other weight control programs. Don't limit yourself to bracelets which may be shunned by men. Why not create key chains or other means for watching those fat grams, carbs, or other annoying weight "uppers" we hate to wear but love to eat. You may try to market these to the actual facilities, where an item of this kind may not exist but would be a great sellable item to those wanting a healthier lifestyle. Be sure to respect copyright or use of names. You don't want to go up against the big guys (no pun intended)!

Renaissance Fairs

Hark, to the Renfaire we go! Many cities have a Renaissance Faire, where you see damsels in distress being saved by knights in shining armor, hear period music, or view the human chess board with a live action game of chess. I love these events because they are so much fun. What a great way to play dress-up and get into character. Because I was unsuccessful in finding a book specifically on Renaissance jewelry, I had to compile a notebook of my own. That was a lot of work! Surprisingly, many of the styles were not too different from today. Beaded jewelry with pendants was common as well as simple focal points strung on silk or leather cord. With brass stampings, you can add ornamental filigree work into your designs, and make them even more authentic-looking by adding a small cabochon or pearl drops. Another unique item to consider would be the Paternosters, which were the forerunners of the modern Catholic and Anglican rosaries.

Setting up a booth at this type of event will require booth rent and being present during the entire event. Many of these fairs last several weeks being in full swing during the weekends only. You will also need to purchase a period costume, as well as a "pavilion" style tent (not the plain white tent you get at big box stores or party warehouses). You may have to be accepted or juried-in to participate, so make sure your pieces are as true to period in design as possible. These fairs are held nationwide, so you may be able to attend others in neighboring states or towns if you are well-located to do so. These are fun events and should be considered if you are willing to put in the time and energy for the initial set-up. It is noteworthy to mention the Society for Creative Anachronism (SCA). Each state has its own listing of societies, and these can be found on the SCA websites. You may want to contact the presidents of these organizations in your area to learn what process you can go through to sell your period pieces to the members of the organization. Renaissance Magazine, which can be purchased at your local book store, lists all the Renaissance Faires in the nation. You can place your own ad with them as well. It's a worthy consideration indeed!

Salons & Spas

As I was walking by a beauty treatment spa one evening, I peeked in the window and saw a gorgeous display of crafted jewelry elegantly placed on a table. As this was a high-end spa, the beautiful jewelry fit right in with the décor. This clued me in to the fact that nice beauty salons and day spas would be places to market your jewelry. Many women are coming in to be pampered and "beautified" and what a better way to finish off the visit than to take home a unique necklace, bracelet, or fun pair of earrings. Speak to the salon or spa owner to see what styles customers would prefer. You can then tailor your designs to fit the needs of the customers who frequent the establishment.

Florist Shops

I met a local florist who showed me a book on bridal decorations. From this book, she had gotten the idea to make some gorgeous table adornments with freshwater pearls, and she was also considering the idea of making jeweled favor boxes. I couldn't help but think what a novel idea this was! If you're pretty crafty, why not think outside the "jewelry" box, so to speak, and create some classy table decorations. A florist in your area may be only too glad to have these wreaths to rent out to customers, and they will make their money back over and over again in rental fees. Jeweled favor boxes will give them another item to offer their customers, who can then tuck in a sweet surprise for a special person in their lives. You could also create these for your customers to purchase when they buy your jewelry. It will be a beautiful way to store their piece.

eBay, Auctions & Stores

I was buying and selling on eBay in 1995, when the company was new and the hottest site on the Internet. It was exciting to list your goods and peep back later to see that people had placed a bid on one or more of your items. Off to the post office I would go, carting tons of boxes on my luggage carrier, which I had purchased at my mother's suggestion. Then later the eBay Store was created, where you could list countless items, choosing to either put them on the auction block or list them for someone to buy outright without going through the bidding process, which can be timely and uncertain. I made some good money when I was selling on eBay, and it was fresh and new at the time I sold my merchandise. I must add that jewelry was not in my listings at the time. Though eBay is still a great place to buy and sell goods, the enthusiasm and novelty it had in the beginning has, in my opinion, become more subdued. There are those who do a good business there, and many still go to the site to buy. If you are selling, you will want to take a hard look at what you want to sell and determine if eBay is really the best avenue for you. In reviewing the jewelry category, I must admit that it is extremely well represented, and I do mean well! However, if you still want to try your hand at selling jewelry on eBay or from an eBay Store, here are some things you should consider before you tackle this venue. First you will have to set up an account with the site and have a credit card on file or set up a PayPal account (which is also owned by eBay) in order to pay your fees. You will have to pay listing and sales fees, though these are still low and allow you to make a nice profit if your items sell.

If you choose to do an eBay Store, you will have to pay a monthly fee to keep it open, as well as pay listing fees for the auction side and sales fees for anything you sell. The monthly fee, though not a bad price, can add up if you are not selling anything. You will then have the pleasure of trying to figure out how to sell your items and complete the appropriate listing forms. Adding pictures to your listing is a good way to help sell your items, but unless you have some web space to store the pictures from where you can upload your files to the listing form, adding a picture can be tricky to figure out. If you choose to set up an eBay Store, then you will have to learn how to navigate the templates used to set up your store and the way you want it to look, regarding color scheme, placement of buttons and category types, to name a few areas. eBay has a host of tools for you to use, but these all come with a fee for each one you choose. Though these add-on fees may appear small at first, it will be amazing to see how quickly they add up, and what started out as affordable, has now become more expensive than you had planned. Another consideration is the time involved in learning how to navigate the system, entering your items, and adding descriptions and pictures. The last part of this task is communicating with buyers, packaging their items, and shipping them out in a timely manner.

One drawback to eBay is that returns are not usually considered, as this site is modeled off traditional auctions. If you attend an auction and secure a winning bid, you are stuck with the item you purchased and you may not return it. Many dealers on eBay work their auctions in this manner, though each dealer can have their own return policy. You will need to determine if you wish to accept returns or not. There are processes to "take back" a bid if someone defaults, but this can be time-consuming. Overall, eBay can be a fun and exciting site to use. You have the potential of meeting some nice people as well as finding other sources for your business. With some practice and understanding of how to use the site, you might have another means for selling your jewelry.

Your Own Website

If you are feeling creative and want the challenge of a big learning curve, try creating your own website. This can be fun but extremely time-consuming. Once you set it up, all you do is make modifications as needed. You will need to obtain a domain name, which is your Internet address so people can find you on the web. In the world of the Internet, there are only a few companies that manage the domain name directories. However, there are several companies that will register your chosen domain name for you. All you need to do is go to their sites, create a name you want, and see if it has been taken by someone else. If not, you are free to use the name. Go Daddy and Network Solutions are a couple of companies who have Internet sites where you can select a domain name. They take care of the registration as well as offer a variety of web hosting programs. You will need a web-hosting program so your site can be posted on the World Wide Web. The next step will be to purchase a website creator package such as Microsoft FrontPage or Dreamweaver, just to name a few. Learning these packages is not as easy as it is made out to be, and you will spend hours trying to learn the features and how they all work together. Once you do figure it all out, you are then ready to take pictures of items and list them on your own site. Launching your site to the Internet will require a user name and password with the hosting company you have selected. It will then be up to you to advertise your site to drive people to it.

For those of you who do not wish to do this on your own or feel a little cyber challenged, you can take advantage of services that build sites for you. Wire-Sculpture.com pairs with a company called Claim the Web. This company will create a site for you and offer support in getting your information and products out on the Internet. For more information on this great service, you can follow this link: www.wire-sculpture.com/business.

Having your own web site in the Age of Information is great, but beware the mentality of "If I build it, they will come." This simply will not work; you will have to work it. Put your web address on every piece of literature you have for your business, pay the fee for Google™ AdWords, and submit your site address to as many search engines as possible. Submitting your website domain name to search engines such as Google or Yahoo allows others to find your site when they type in certain keywords. There are several free companies on the internet that will allow you to submit your domain name to several search engines at a time. All you will have to do is complete their form and push a "Submit" button and your site will be listed in 60 to 90 days or more. To go into the jargon of the computer world and try to explain every term for web site creation and launching is beyond the scope of this book. For those of you who have some understanding, you know what I mean. Another idea worth considering is placing your items for sale on some of the craft sites that are specifically designed for selling handcrafted items. An Internet search or one of the beading/wire magazines will provide some good resources for this. The downside is that these sites take a percentage of your sales, as well as charge you listing fees. But they are a wonderful way to have a web presence.

Subleasing Space

You may want to consider subleasing space in another shop owned by someone else. Sometimes the owners are willing to sublease shelf or floor space. The nice deal with this arrangement is that you don't have to be there to sell the merchandise, because the shop owner will be able to do that for you. The drawback is that you do have to pay a monthly rental fee and most likely a percentage of the sales back to the owner. You are in business after all, so these fees will be part of your business expenses. However, you will have a shop location where customers and travelers can view and purchase your items. This is a great way to have your jewelry in an actual retail store, which can add legitimacy to your business.

Your Own Jewelry Boutique

This idea is only for the serious-minded, and not for the faint-at-heart! Unless you are committed to selling as a business, have the bank account to support it, and the willingness to work hard, don't even think about this one! You can be the shop owner, and let others sublease from you. Depending on where you live and the retail space available, you may be able to rent space at a rate that might fit your pocket book. If you can get equally committed artisans to pay rent to place their items in your shop, you may be able to have a nice artisan shop where consumers can enjoy purchasing beautiful and unique items. Determine if the landlord allows subleasing, keeping in mind that you will need to cover the rent should you not have other participants (or few participants) at any given time. There are a host of issues to address when being a shop owner, and I'm not covering them here. I am merely planting a seed in the mind of the next would-be entrepreneur!

Marketing at a Glance

Specialty Areas	Owner	Address	Venue Type

Chapter Eight
Spilling the Beans: On Marketing Your Jewelry

Here comes the part where many people fall off the bandwagon—don't you be one of them! Marketing is not for everyone, and this issue was noted in an earlier chapter, but what I want to address in this section is a little more detail on the how-to's once you have decided where you want to go and whom to approach. Though my aim is not to cover every facet of marketing in this book, there are some very good sources where you can gain insight into more effective sales and marketing techniques. If you want to learn more about getting the appointment and getting past gate-keepers you may consider reading some books on actual sales and marketing techniques, such as Jeffrey Gitomer's Little Red Book of Selling, Little Red Book of Sales Answers, Little Gold Book of Yes! Attitude, and Little Green Book of Getting Your Way. There are some good points made in these books, and you will be able to apply them relevantly to many aspects of your marketing tasks. You will learn why customers buy, why customer loyalty is priceless, and how you can overcome some basic problems faced in sales and marketing. You also learn how to keep a positive attitude as well as how to address customer concerns. These books are also concise, clear, and easy to read. Unless you are willing to market and stay on top of it, your business may be just a glorified hobby. Below are some tips and suggestions on how to tackle this. As your business grows and you gain confidence, hopefully, your marketing ability will mature so that you are not afraid to approach different parties to talk about what you have to offer them. Your business will grow and so will you as a person!

Letting the Cat Out of the Canister:
Creating Your Marketing Plan

My first suggestion is the development of a marketing plan. A plan contains many areas that are addressed: sales goals, situational analysis, competition issues, sales strategies, and a host of other things. It's overwhelming when you look at all the pieces you have to dissect and analyze. However, you need to have a marketing plan, even if it is a scaled-down version of what you may see in marketing textbooks or on the Internet. When I had a marketing-type job during one of my corporate experiences, I had to create a marketing plan – outlining my goals for the next quarter, as well as contacts I would call upon. I had to look at my competition and I had to look at how much business I could potentially get from the contacts I was considering. The bottom line is: you have to know who and where your contacts are. You also have to evaluate your competition and see what you offer that is different.

Finally, you will have to determine if your prospective contacts are a source of business for you. You will need to note sales goals for each of these contacts or outline which types of jewelry you want to sell and to whom. Note your marketing strategies and include shows and other venues as part of your marketing activities. For example, you may want to outline your contact list on a per quarter basis. If you start in January and go through March, list the contacts you will see in January, February, and then March. Continue in this manner until you have your calendar complete. Your contacts need to include those that are just follow-ups versus those that are new. This insures you don't miss anyone and allows you to see your vendors on a regular basis. You will then be able to note if they need any more items from you or if you need to try another style with them. Meeting new contacts will give you more options to sell your jewelry as well as provide you with back-up accounts if other avenues drop off. Even if someone decides not to buy your line today, you may ask their opinion regarding which styles they did like. Setting goals for sales amounts or for certain jewelry types is a must. You have to have a clear idea of what you want to achieve when you meet with people. I have a friend who told me that when she sells during a given day, she chooses certain items she wants to see move from the shelf or rack. During the day, she directs customers to those items, while trying to fit these in with their needs or to merely inform them that these choices are available. You may want to do that with your pieces. Suggest other articles to your accounts or try to be creative and see if you can make a product that fits in specifically with their shop. When I sold bridal jewelry, I specifically went into the shops to match colors of beads to certain gowns that were going to be sold that season. In this way, the jewelry matched the gowns and had a higher chance of being sold, especially as an ensemble. You may want to list your accounts and note the types of items specific to that owner's shop. Note styles or colors to help serve as a reminder. A hip boutique will have different styles of jewelry than a child's shop or a bridal shop.

Thanks a Latte: Marketing Etiquette

The trickiest obstacle you may encounter will be actually getting in contact with the owner. You always want to speak to the decision-makers since they are the ones who will be paying your bills and selecting which of your pieces will make it into their shop. As you make your list of contacts, determine the owner of the establishment and find out the best time to set up an appointment. Though it is possible they may have a chance to see you on-the-spot if you just walk into their shop, it's not likely. I always spoke with the owners first to inquire of their interest in the pieces I created. Once they expressed an affirmative and positive reaction, I set up an appointment to actually show them the lines I had created. From that moment, they either purchased pieces that were already created, or I made up pieces "to order" based on clothing style and color or other special requests. I would receive a check for payment at the end of the meeting. In cases where I was dropping off specified pieces, a check would be waiting where the amount could be filled in by the manager acting on the owner's behalf.

Café Chatter: Talk the Talk

Speaking directly to the owners and their little group of staff is one level of communication. You usually know the people involved and you begin to establish a professional "friendship." It's comfortable to go into the shop and strike up a conversation or discuss the new items that might be of interest to them. What do you do when you are at a show and everyone is a stranger? People are coming to you, and now you're in charge. One of the first things to do is smile and say, "Hello!" You want to build some form of positive rapport as quickly as possible as people at shows are quickly going from one table to another, and usually won't linger like they will in an actual shop. Ask them if there is a particular item they are looking for. Do they need a gift for someone else or do they want to treat themselves to a nice piece you've made? If they are eyeing a particular item but seem to be waffling, try to find out just why that is. Their concern is a key to being able to make the sale or not. They need to feel that purchasing your bracelet or necklace will make them feel good about themselves or they can accessorize with it in several different ways. Sometimes I'll joke with a customer and state, "This piece would really like a new home because it's really getting tired of being with me." I usually get a smile, and many times the customer ends up buying the piece. Be willing to discuss custom-making an item if the customer doesn't see a particular color they like, but they like the over-all style of something. Find out what they do and what activities they engage in. You may be able to make something special just for them. This is all a form of marketing to your customer while they are in your presence. These activities are not just solely for people who are cold-calling or involved in other types of sales. You are always marketing whether it's engaging in a conversation with someone, being aware of how you display your items at a show or whether you are truly out making contacts for future accounts. Sell it like you mean it!

No Sitting on the Back Burner: Be Prepared

One lady I met a few years ago was wearing a really cute onyx pendant heart with some wire swirls around it. The pendant was the focal point for a pretty strand of matching beads. When I commented on her piece, she indicated she had made it herself. She went on to note that she actually sold quite a few of her pieces to people who saw her wearing her own jewelry. Furthermore, she indicated that she carried a special case in the trunk of her car containing several pieces that people could buy from her immediately on sight. When I heard her story, I couldn't help but remark to myself that she had a cool idea. What a novel way to make sales! She was her own best form of advertising. To bring my point home, I know a lady who went on vacation one summer. She took with her all the jewelry pieces she had created, which consisted of everything from crocheted bracelets to knotted tin-cup style necklaces. She informed me that during her time on this vacation she sat by the pool and worked on new pieces. Because she had jewelry on display, people wandered up to her inquiring if they could purchase certain pieces. She sold over three hundred dollars worth of her jewelry! Therefore, always have your jewelry on display! If you're not too in love with it, sell it if someone is willing to buy it from you! I once teased an artist friend of mine by calling her a jewelry whore because she would sell any of her work for a price! She laughed and readily agreed, stating that she could always make something else newer and better. Carry a jewelry roll in your car, and be ready in some way to showcase what you have, and sell, sell, sell! People love immediate gratification, and so will you when it's money in your pocket. There are a few other marketing and advertising considerations you may want to keep in mind. These can help build and maintain your business and pay off in the long run. I'll review some of them here.

Who's On Your Menu? Lead Lists

These lists are just that – lead customers who may want to buy what you have to sell. There are companies that are solely in the business to build and collect lead lists to sell for hundreds of dollars to businesses wanting to reach a large potential market base. You may not want to pay lots of money to get addresses for nearby zip codes, but you can create your own lead list. For example, any time you participate in a show, have a sheet ready for someone to fill out their name and associated contact information, as well as their birth and anniversary date. Ensure them that their information will be kept private and will not be shared with or sold to anyone. The reason you are collecting this information is to inform them of your show schedule as well as to include them in any correspondence you may send out in the future. Get a calendar and organize people's birth and anniversary dates by month and send out a group email indicating that you know this special date is near and that you have some items in which they will be interested. You can also include holidays as times to correspond with customers. In this way, you have a reason to always keep reminding them of you and what you have to offer. You are a designer, so offer your services as one!

Flavors of the Day: Web Newsletters

This is a wonderful way to keep in contact with your customers. Create a quarterly (maybe monthly) newsletter telling your customers about any new items you've created, as well as where you may be having a show in the near future. Because many traditional Internet email accounts block the sending of bulk email (due to spamming issues), there are companies that are set up to let one send bulk mail without any server issues. Constant Contact® is one of several of these companies. They offer tutorials on how to use their service as well as provide templates for your use. You can also upload your logo or other graphics to spruce up your newsletter. They also provide the recipient with an opt out feature should they no longer wish to continue receiving your communications. Using this service myself, I highly recommend it. You pay for this service based on the number of people you have in your contact list and it is very affordable. It's amazing to see the results you can obtain from sending out a reminder to your customers. Try a promotion of some kind, perhaps giving away a simple pair of earrings with the purchase of a necklace or bracelet. You may set a dollar amount for a purchase to receive a free gift. In my experience, I find that offering a free gift with a purchase is an effective marketing strategy which usually entices many customers to buy. People seem to enjoy receiving a gift for a purchase they have made. Overall, newsletters help legitimize your business and remind customers that you are still out there. Collecting their information automatically gets their permission to be contacted.

What's On the Board? Other Advertising Venues

There are other routes for advertising without having to spend thousands of dollars for high-end fashion magazine ads. If your community has local periodicals focusing on local events and news, you can sometimes place an ad at a more affordable cost. Having a web presence for reference will help boost your sales because the prospective customer can get online and actually see what you have to offer. Make sure the ad shows a great piece you've made. You want to attract attention. Try obtaining permission to post a flyer or ad post card on college bulletin boards, and office park boards. You may want to create flyers to give to individual businesses where they can hand them out to workers in their establishment. Perhaps a kind administrative assistant may be willing to help with this. Possibilities are endless; you just have to be bold and creative.

A Few Last Drops: Last Minute Talking Points

There are a few housekeeping issues to address which may help you as you market and build your business. Though you try to cover your bases, it's difficult to think of everything right off the top of your head. You will sometimes have to live and learn as you encounter different experiences when catering to people. I review a few subjects here. After that, you're on your own!

Will That Be for Here or to Go?
Consignment vs. Buy Outright

Most of you will no doubt find that many shops will just want to put your jewelry on consignment, meaning they will not pay you until your items sell. This puts the artist in the hot seat because the shop owner has your merchandise in their shop; and they did not have to pay for it. If your product sells, then you get paid. If not, there's no loss on part of the shop owner. A friend of mine who is a shop owner once told me that she steers away from consignment. Her argument was that first, she believed the artist needed to be paid for his or her time and merchandise. Second, she as the owner had no incentive in selling items in her shop that she had not paid for. To her, it was a win/win situation if the artist got paid first, and the owner then felt an incentive to sell merchandise in which they had invested. After she made her point, I have since tried to avoid consignment. Here's how I did it. When asked if I would leave items on consignment, I usually said to the owner (politely of course!) that I tried to avoid consignment because my merchandise usually did better if there was an investment by the owner to sell it. They can always put it on sale if the piece doesn't work, and they won't lose anything. Also, I mentioned that there was no minimum purchase amount, so they would not have to tie up large amounts of money with merchandise that was new to them. Usually, they would end up buying several pieces. If an owner insists on consignment, you will want to ask the following:

1. How will I be paid?
2. How will they keep up with what has sold?
3. How will theft or breakage be handled?

Based on their answers, you can decide if a consignment arrangement is best with this particular shop. Antique malls are fantastic for consignment arrangements, because they have excellent systems for tracking items sold and know what to pay the vendors. Smaller shops and boutiques may not be so savvy. Again, I would recommend the owner buying outright, but if you have to do consignment, know their system and how you will get your money. Engaging in consignment is always riskier for the designer than the owner. You have put time into creating your pieces as well as money into purchasing the materials. Also, you have received no money for your merchandise. You will have no control over loss, theft, or breakage, and getting your money can prove to be a daunting task if you deal with a consignment shop whose reputation is a negative one. Proceed with caution.

Two for One: Trade-Outs

There is the question of trade-outs if items don't sell. Unfortunately, I had to learn the hard way, and I still feel a little bad to this day based on my personal experiences with this issue. It is easy to indicate that you will be willing to trade out pieces that don't sell. This usually encourages owners to feel they are taking less of a risk in buying your merchandise. The down side is when you are suddenly asked to replace several items they have purchased with new ones. In my situation the number of items ended up being eighteen! Unfortunately, I was not able to re-do all those pieces, and most likely the owner ended up putting the other items on sale. The problem was that we did not discuss early in our dealings what trade out meant regarding the number of pieces. She and I both had high hopes for all the pieces I made, and she approved every one of them before purchasing. However, we found out later that her clientele appeared to prefer one style heavily over the other, and so she wanted me to exchange out the styles piece by piece. Doing that would have made me lose big time on this deal, especially in regard to labor. My advice is: determine the number of items you are willing to trade out and set a limit on how many times you will do this before you and the owner decide that perhaps your line is just not working for them. In the end, my shop owner had decided that there were too many pieces of jewelry in her shop that competed with mine. Therefore, we decided to end the relationship, and I moved on to other venues.

Do You Have Something Stronger? Returns

Nobody likes to have something returned to them, and this is a big pet peeve of mine. However, you don't want your customer to get stuck with something they don't like. If a customer returns a piece, you may decide to be a little more forgiving and make the changes, depending on how extensive they are. Charging a small labor fee may be helpful to cover your time. How you prevent or minimize returns in the first place should be the real question. You may want to think about a return policy or lack thereof on ready-made jewelry that you sell. If you are designing a piece especially for someone's event, sit down with this person and suggest some ideas or draw out some designs that they approve of. Last of all, let the customer know up front what your policies and charges are for everything so they are not blind-sided and think you tried to be dishonest. If a customer is returning a broken piece they just purchased from you, determine what happened to it. If it appears that it merely fell apart, and there was no undue handling, you may be obligated to fix the piece free of charge just to maintain a good relationship with the customer. Sit down and think about your policies and how you wish to handle them. You may have them printed on small sheets of paper to be handed to the customer along with their receipt of purchase. Trust me;

you'll be glad you did. Having a good policy helps prevent or at least minimize what can be a potentially nasty situation later.

Check, Please! Methods of Payment

Payment is the bread and butter of your business. Without it, you don't have a business. What kinds of payment forms should you take or not take? Cash is always good. There's no charge for using it, and there are no fees you have to pay for using a service, such as credit card processing. You don't have to worry about the funds being rejected! Then of course, there are credit cards. Because of so many home-based businesses and those involving selling at shows, you can now have accounts that let you have terminals that are wireless so you can process from anywhere, or you can simply log onto a computer and type in the customer information. Authorize.Net® is a great company that lets you use your computer as your credit card terminal. Having used them in a previous business, I highly recommend them. All you have to do is collect the customer's name, billing address, phone number, credit card number, expiration date, and CVV number on the back of the card. You can also put in their email address so they get a confirmation notice that their card was charged. If you do the transactions after a show or other sales venture, you may risk a card getting rejected. You can always run the card through again at a later date or make a phone call to the customer for assistance. Keep in mind there are transaction and charge-back fees as well. It's all worth it due to the amount of sales you can process. People usually don't carry much cash these days and taking credit cards is handy for most.

Checks are always tricky. Though I've experienced a few returned checks in my time, I've always been able to collect on them quickly. Most of the time, I have no problems with them. Keep in mind that some people do make mistakes in calculating their bank account, or that they may be thinking you won't cash or deposit their check as quickly as you do. Due to the digital age we live in, transactions get posted a little more quickly than we had counted on. It's up to you to decide to take checks or not. If they are local, you can always go to a customer's branch bank to try to cash out. If the customer is out of state, you can always contact their bank to see if funds are available and then take a chance by running the check through again. The down side is that you are charged a fee for the return. Keep in mind that the customer got charged much higher than you did! If you can't get collection on a check, there are local collection agencies that can be of assistance. If the amount was not too high, you may just have to write the transaction off as a loss. Spending too much time and energy after a while can end up making it not worth your effort.

Let's Blow This Joint! You Can Shop Too

Last of all, you can shop, too. What does this mean? This means that while you think you and your jewelry are at the mercy of being accepted by a shop owner, you actually can make a decision that you don't want your merchandise in a particular shop. If you have a contact down on your list, and you don't like what you see when you actually visit them, don't put your merchandise there. I have a friend who states that she evaluates the shop as much as they evaluate her lines. If she sees a shop that is poorly displayed, has poor lighting, is in a bad location, or whose merchandise is poorly selected, she takes her totes and heads straight for the door! She's very wary of someone with a bad reputation for not paying or who cheats their vendors. She also looks at how she is treated when she goes in. If she feels the staff is unfriendly and are not inclined to sell the shop, chances are they won't sell her line; she won't do business with them. Keep in mind that you can accept or reject a shop as well as they can do the same to you. You want a great working relationship with the owner of a nicely located, beautifully stocked shop. After all, you are in business together.

Marketing Plan

Coverage Period
From: _____ To: _____

Top New Contacts to be Visited for This Period

Name	Address	Owner

Established Contacts to be Visited This Period

Name	Address	Owner

Mission for New Contacts

Name	Mission	Results

Events/Shows for This Period

Name	Address	Date

Overall Sales Goals For This Period:

_____

_____

_____

Jewelry Types to be Sold:

_____

_____

_____

Competition Issues:

_____

_____

_____

Situational Issues:

_____

_____

_____

Client Profile

(You will need to create a profile for each customer on your list.)

Account Name:

_____

Address:

_____

Owner/President/Director:

_____

Specialty Areas:

_____

Items Requested:

_____

Contact Dates

_____

Design Contract

(This contract lists your customer's personal contact information as well as outlines what you have planned for them. Note here design ideas, colors, styles, size, and other special requests that your customer would like to see in what you create for them.)

Date: _____

Customer Name: _____

Address: _____

Phone Number: _____

Jewelry Type: ___Necklace ___Bracelet ___Earrings ___Other

Other (if selected above): _____

Size: _____

Colors: _____

Medium (Wire, PMC, etc.): _____

_____

Price: _____

Down Payment: _____

Other Requests: _____

Delivery Date: _____

Client Signature: _____

Return Policy

Think about your personal feelings in regard to returns. Do you believe all sales are final? Why or Why Not?

_____

_____

Will you charge a fee of some kind if you have to make a change on a piece of jewelry that was purchased as is? If so, how much?
$_____

Are you willing to repair jewelry you made that broke?

_____

Will you charge for this? _____ If so, how much?

_____

How will you handle customer dissatisfaction with a piece that you designed especially for their needs?

_____

_____

_____

Will you charge an additional fee for design time? _____

If so, how much? $ _____

If not, why not? _____

_____

My Return Policy Is:

_____

Chapter Nine
Espresso Kick: Principles and Elements of Design

Though this book was created to address selling jewelry as a business, I thought it would be helpful to briefly discuss some art and design principles and elements that can help you as you create your lines. After all, without creating something, you have nothing to sell! First of all, the basic principles of design lay down the foundation or framework to help guide the artist in composing their piece, whether it be a painting, architectural layout, or a piece of jewelry. These principles are not just a single factor, but several that tie in together upon completion. No matter what you are trying to create, you will keep these principles in mind so that your final project possesses a total look that is pleasing to the viewer. Basic design elements are those individual aspects or "pieces" that reflect the principles, and do so harmoniously. Now I'll explain further what these framework components and aspects are.

Basic Design Principles

The following terms are those you will see when studying the design process for many art forms. They are consistent and determined to be the guiding points for creating skillful and effective work.

Emphasis: Emphasis is the use of a focal point to draw the eye to a certain location or in certain directions as you view a finished piece. Focal points such as pendants are often used for emphasis in necklaces. Bracelets may contain certain color schemes or figures in the center so that the emphasis is on the top of the wrist. Earrings may sport figures or drops. You can also create emphasis by using shapes and colors in sequence at certain points of a piece so that the eye falls on that section when viewing. Areas of emphasis create "pop" when the eye views them.

Balance: Balance is usually described as the use of light and dark elements to create an even look. But I find that this concept goes beyond just mere light and dark. When you are viewing a finished product, there are several aspects affecting the total look. To view this another way, there are ways a piece can appear incongruent and hit the viewer as "rather funny" or as something odd and just not right. For example, if you place certain bead shapes, cabochons, and focal pieces haphazardly with no thought to the effect they create, your piece may appear "lop-sided" or incongruent. The viewer's eyes may not be pulled into a certain flow which should occur when you view a piece of art. A piece that is balanced has a harmonious flow and look, with focal points that pull the eyes in certain directions throughout. The overall effect when viewing the work should leave one with a pleasurable feeling and not with one of something gone awry. For example, I crafted an Art Deco-inspired wire necklace, where one side was bundled square wire with crystals, and the other side was two crafted "chains" made of crystal connections. A focal piece was added, and when you looked at the completed piece, both sides of the necklace were balanced with a more solid piece on one side and double strands for an illusion of "thickness" on the other.

Rhythm: Rhythm is the pattern or repetition you see throughout a piece. For example, a repeated pattern of two red beads followed by one black bead, establishes rhythm because it shows off a visual cadence. Rhythmic pieces are classic and popular and are found many times when crafting symmetrical jewelry. If done skillfully, even asymmetrical jewelry can have a unique rhythm, especially when using shape combinations and color arrangement to achieve a certain look. But remember, even an asymmetrical piece should have overall balance when it is viewed. When creating wire pieces, for example, you may have 5 bindings on a bundle of square wire followed with a bead, 5 more bindings followed by another bead, et cetera.

Contrast: Contrast is the use of different shapes and colors throughout a piece. This concept goes hand-in-hand with balance because lack of contrast may make a piece appear incongruent or at the very least uninteresting. Use of color and shape are some simple means of achieving contrast. Placing a smaller round black bead next to a large green square one is an effective way of creating contrast through use of different shapes and color combinations. If you make chandelier earrings, you can achieve contrast through use of the connecting component, attachment of dangles, and perhaps the use of chain. You further create contrast within the earrings by the use of different bead shapes and colors. In the end you will have a looped component with its unique shape and the dangles which provide motion to the overall piece.

Unity: Unity is the overall look of a piece where the placement of certain items, and the use of others, all create a solid and completed look when finished. When an object shows unity, the focal points are easily discernable, colors and shapes flow, and the overall look is harmonious. In the end the finished product looks "pulled together."

Basic Design Elements

These terms will be encountered when addressing design elements which are the actual building blocks reflecting the design principles. When composed correctly in a project, the designer will have a work of art that stands out and merits attention.

Line: This term indicates directionality, meaning horizontal, vertical, or diagonal. Most jewelry contains horizontal and vertical lines, given that rings, necklaces, and bracelets go around a form, meaning fingers, necks, and wrists. Verticalness occurs through the use of dangles or drops that hang down from the main unit of a piece. Other directionality can be achieved through bead shapes or stone patterns which in effect can create a line when placed with other similar beads. With products rendered in wire, you see a variety of directions from diagonal to zigzag as well as the usual horizontal and vertical. Use of these differing directions is what gives wire pieces their funky uniqueness or classic sleekness.

Shape: Shape is the outline of an object which usually represents the common forms, such as circles, squares, rectangles, ovals, and triangles. Other shapes include cubes and diamonds (bicones). Beads definitely embody all the shapes you can imagine, and using these in creative combinations within your wire projects lead to some beautiful jewelry.

Texture: The visual and tactile pattern on a given surface is known as its texture. If you look at gemstones and different Czech glass you may see a variety of swirls, stripes, or animal-type prints on the bead. Many Lampwork beads have raised areas on them to create an even more obvious texture – one where the effect is tactile as well as visual. Wire jewelry can contain different textures as well, such as the sleekness gained from bundled square wire. Twisted wire provides a filigree look, while other features, such as rosettes, can add swirly looks to your pieces. Combining these effects create striking, fun pieces. Texture becomes an even more important "player" in design, because if the components are placed together without regard, you will easily have a "busy" looking piece, where focal points may become "invisible" and get lost in the patterns. Overall, the design proves to be ineffective in achieving a pleasing look, and the viewer quickly tires of the piece.

Direction: Direction is the overall motion or movement evoked by a piece, especially in regards to how the eye follows certain points throughout. Chandelier earrings or a necklace with dangles tend to draw the eyes downward. Necklaces that have one strand coming down the neck on one side and then splitting off into multiple strands as they ascend the other side will create a eye motion of right or left, depending on how the necklace is worn. The use of direction in combination with color schemes can create powerful and dazzling jewelry, making a finished necklace, for example, a memorable one.

Color: Colors comprise the different hues created by the primary, secondary and tertiary combinations of red, yellow, and blue. Effective use of color and understanding how contrast works, will allow the artist to create pieces with that "something extra." A viewer may not quite be able to put their finger on it, but something about jewelry with striking color contrasts tends to hold one's attention. Better yet, a customer may feel more compelled to purchase the piece.

Those with Metal Allergies

As a designer there are many populations for which you can create fun and attractive pieces. There does, however, seem to be a small group who has difficulty in finding jewelry to wear. Their problem stems from the fact that when their skin comes into contact with metals, they end up with a terrible rash. Many times the reason for the breakout is due to nickel leaching out of the metal and onto their skin, causing a reaction. Unfortunately, many of the findings used in crafting jewelry contain nickel as the base metal or has this element incorporated as an alloy which is a blend of two or more metals. Even sterling silver (which can be easily worn by most people) can contain some nickel in the alloy, thus, setting off an allergic reaction in one who has severe metal allergies. As a designer you luckily have an arsenal up your sleeve and can make pieces that can be safely worn!

First, you can address the findings issue directly, and use metals made of Titanium or Niobium. Because these metals contain no alloy, there are no other elements that can leach out into the skin. Like everything else that is specialized, there is a cost associated with using these metals. Titanium and Niobium can be pricey in certain forms, and it may be difficult to retrieve your costs when using these in your jewelry you wish to sell. Do keep them in mind, because they can be a resource if you need to develop some pieces for those with severe allergic reactions to metal.

Chapter Ten
One for the Road! Conclusion

I have now concluded my presentation to you of ideas on how to jumpstart your business. After reading this book, you will want to consider beginning your business in selling a product you love most – your own jewelry designs! Whether you pursue selling your pieces as a hobby or full-time business, I hope these ideas I have presented jolt your thinking towards creative sales and marketing techniques that work for you! Being in business for yourself can be extremely rewarding and offer you many freedoms, such as being your own boss, being in charge of your workday schedule, and determining how you want to pursue your endeavors. Nobody can block you or hold you back. You are the decision-maker! Though you have some new freedoms, you also have some responsibilities, such as marketing, producing merchandise, organizing your time to fill orders, working with customers, and a host of other duties discussed previously. Overall, you must have a love of business and have an entrepreneurial spirit and drive to make this venture successful. You have to find ways to sell your jewelry to such a degree and price point in order to cover business expenses and make a salary you need or want.

Selling and marketing is a numbers game, and the more you work it, the better you will become at selling your jewelry designs. No one knows this better than a lady I know in my community. Because she is also a Nashville resident, I have personally seen her booths at several shows throughout the years. She has her pieces in many shops, including a museum gift shop! Continually marketing her business, she generates enough revenue to sell her jewelry full time! She works every show and venue she can, and actively seeks ways to keep her business out in the public eye. She indicates that she markets and sells her designs any chance that comes her way and is always looking for a new opportunity to show off her work to potential customers. Loving what she does, she is a good businessperson, knowing what it takes to make it work. What an inspiration! Seeing her in action brings home the importance of commitment and the pay-offs you can reap! You are in a position to make someone happy with what you create. Your beautiful work gives pleasure to the recipients. You in turn receive satisfaction and reward knowing that you have contributed to the emotions of so many that love your creations.

Making jewelry is very therapeutic for those who derive joy from it. I've heard these comments from so many people and I've experienced it myself – that's why I believe it. Most of all, you too will derive pleasure from being in business and taking on the challenges that go with it. It is my wish for you in using this book as your guide that you create a business for yourself in which you can be happy and satisfied with what you achieve. Work through any struggles you may have because perseverance only brings success. I may not be present to see you succeed in your endeavors, but when you do, I hope I can be there in spirit. I wish my best to all of you!

Appendix & Resources

Appendix
Wire Chart

Precious Metals Wire
(Approximate Feet per Troy Ounce)

Gauge	Gold Filled Round	Gold Filled Square	Gold Filled Half Round	Sterling Round	Sterling Square	Sterling Half Round
14	5.45	4.29	11.08	4.72	3.71	9.83
16	8.65	6.81	16.83	7.52	5.91	13.50
18	13.97	11.00	27.33	11.90	9.35	24.66
20	21.82	17.18	38.50	18.98	14.91	41.00
21	27.59	21.72	51.00	23.92	18.79	54.00
22	34.75	27.72	70.75	30.21	23.73	60.75
24	55.87	44.00		47.85	37.58	
26	87.33	68.79		76.34	59.96	
28	140.77	110.84		121.21	95.20	
30	223.71	176.15		193.05	151.62	
32	349.65	275.31		306.75	240.92	

Note: Measurements are approximate and may vary by mill.

Copper and Brass Wire (Feet/Pound)

Gauge	Copper/Brass Round	Copper/Brass Square
10	31.82	25.05
12	50.59	39.83
14	80.44	63.33
16	127.9	100.71
18	203.4	160.16
20	323.4	254.65
21	407.8	321.10
22	514.2	404.88
24	817.7	643.86
26	1300	1023.62
28	2067	1627.56
30	3287	2588.19
32	5277	4115.75
34	8310	6543.31

Note: Measurements are approximate and may vary by mill.

Resources

1. Festival Network Online: Lists craft shows, art festivals and fairs in US and Canada, since 1996. www.festivalnet.com
2. Crafts Fair Guide List of Reviewed Shows: Lists, craft festivals in CA, WA, OR, and NV that are listed and reviewed in the Crafts Fair Guide. www.craftsfairguide.com
3. The Crafts Fair Online: Magazines, Journals & Resources Of Interest To Craftspeople. www.craftsfaironline.com/Publications.html
4. Craft Shop Mall Directory: General Directory of Craft Faires, Shows, and Craft Vendors. www.craftshopmall.com/shopping
5. Arrowmont School of Arts and Crafts: Offers instruction in a wide variety of areas, from painting to stained glass. www.arrowmont.org
6. Appalachian Center for Craft: Offers training in a wide variety of craft studies. You can receive a degree or merely become certified in a particular medium without seeking a degree. This center is an extension of Tennessee Tech University. www.tntech.edu/craftcenter/home
7. Dale Armstrong: National designer and artist; offering intensive wire artistry classes in her private studio and is a guest teacher at Stardust Designs Bead Shoppe in Nashville, TN. She also teaches periodically at other locations throughout the nation. See her website for more details. www.cougarscreations.com
8. US Copyright Office: For copyright protection of your designs and work. www.copyright.gov
9. Microstamp: Specializes in creating die stamps to use on blank jewelry tags. Add your name or motif. Just email them a JPG image. They also sell the tags. www.microstampusa.com
10. Web Hosting and Domain Registration Sites: These sites assist you in creating and selecting a domain name and registering this name with the appropriate databases. You can also purchase hosting programs from these companies. www.claimtheweb.com www.godaddy.com www.networksolutions.com
11. Etsy.com: This is a site where all crafts are welcome. Set up an account and begin uploading your products to sell online. www.etsy.com
12. Web Newsletters: Constant Contact®. This company allows you to send bulk email correspondence for a fee based on the number of contacts you have in your account. They offer a tutorial to show how the service works. There are templates to use and an ability to upload logos or other graphics to include in your copy. This is a great service. www.constantcontact.com
13. Web Credit Card Processing: Authorize.Net. This company allows for on-line processing of credit cards. Their site is secure and allows safe transactions. www.authorize.net

14. Renaissance Faires and the SCA: These are wonderful outlets for marketing Medieval and Renaissance jewelry. **www.sca.org**
15. Renaissance Magazine: An historical magazine reviewing anything pertaining to subjects from the dark ages to the Renaissance period. One can place ads for any merchandise they are selling which pertains to these periods in history. **www.renaissancemagazine.com**
16. Underhill Pavilions: Specializing in Renaissance Pavilion tents for Ren Faires. **www.underhillpavilions.com/pavilions.html**
17. Stardust Beads: Online catalog for a wide range of beading supplies as well as insightful books on business and design. **www.stardustbeads.com**
18. Wire-Sculpture: Online source for jewelry wire, tools, beads, cabs, and of course, Dale Cougar Armstrong's instructional DVDs for all levels of wire artists. **www.wire-sculpture.com** Special Business Resource Center: **www.wire-sculpture.com/business**

About the Author

Coming from a line of small business owners on both sides of the family, Mitzi McCartha finally took the plunge and became her own boss after opening her first retail bead shop in 2005. Having worked as a nurse for eighteen years, it was time to make a change. Three previous years of beading as a hobbyist soon turned into an idea that opening a bead shop would allow for fun in both the business and jewelry designing aspects.

Opening a shop was not her first experience in dabbling with small business. Her first encounter in the retail world began in 1995; it included selling gifts and antiques in local antique malls. After five years in the antique's industry, the next venture focused on a service-oriented business, wedding video production. Two years of lugging around heavy video equipment became rather burdensome, and this endeavor came to an end. A brief hiatus ensued, but it was not long until the entrepreneur bug bit again. Never would she dream of a business in beading. Who ever heard of such a thing! Nevertheless, the attempts to create a calorie counting bracelet for use in Weight Watchers® was the springboard for the greatest career move of her life.

Starting out as a hobbyist, and making bridal jewelry for a couple of local bridal shops, the desire to create a full-time business became even stronger. Visualizing the end goal, a business that could be fun as well as profitable, Stardust Designs Bead Shoppe was born. Located in Nashville, Tennessee, Stardust Designs Bead Shoppe is a full service bead store, offering jewelry design classes, as well as a host of glass and gemstone beads and findings. Many customers come in not only to buy beading materials and to take classes, but to also get advice on how to sell their jewelry!